The disciples left everything to follo
so much more than they had already
same adventure – to find a life truly
Jenny Baker, Director of the Sophia Ne

I love this book. I felt challenged, inspired and provoked – often on the same page. A must read for anyone wanting to go deeper in their faith and understanding.
Gavin Calver, National Director Youth for Christ

In a time where young people are looking for something real in their lives that can make a difference, *RISE* helps them to understand that following Jesus is radical. Jason and Rachel Gardner are able to take you on a journey of choices and decisions that could really help you to become who you were created to be.
Richard Dawson, Director, Nottingham YfC

RISE will change your life. It does what it says on the cover. It will cause your faith levels, your knowledge of God, eyebrows and laughter levels all to *RISE*. Jason and Rachel are experienced youth workers whose readable style, engaging story telling, provocative questions and relevant imagery will keep you reading from start to finish.
Phil and Dani Knox, Youth for Christ

As young people embark on an exciting faith adventure it's essential that they have something inspiring, honest, and challenging to help them along the way. In their own inimitable style Rachel and Jason have delivered something that perfectly fits the bill. Essential packing in the faith-journey rucksack.
Matt Summerfield, Urban Saints

Discovering how to make the most of your life has got to be a top priority, and this book will help you do just that. Packed with great insights and illustrations, *RISE* brings the adventure of following Jesus to life in a creative and compelling way. A MUST read for any teenager who wants to walk the talk and challenge those around them to do the same!

Pete Wynter, Director, Onelife

rise

One Life. One Way. One Master

Jason & Rachel Gardner

ivp

INTER-VARSITY PRESS
Norton Street, Nottingham NG7 3HR, England
Email: ivp@ivpbooks.com
Website: www.ivpbooks.com

First published 2011

British Library Cataloguing in Publication Data
A catalogue record for this book is available from the British Library.

ISBN: 978-1-84474-504-3

Set in Myriad 10/12pt
Typeset in Great Britain by CRB Associates, Potterhanworth, Lincolnshire
Printed and bound in Great Britain by Ashford Colour Press Ltd, Gosport, Hampshire

Inter-Varsity Press publishes Christian books that are true to the Bible and that communicate the gospel, develop discipleship and strengthen the church for its mission in the world.

Inter-Varsity Press is closely linked with the Universities and Colleges Christian Fellowship, a student movement connecting Christian Unions in universities and colleges throughout Great Britain, and a member movement of the International Fellowship of Evangelical Students. Website: www.uccf.org.uk

Dedication

This book is dedicated to our parents, who have taught us how to live the best life,

and to Roxanne, Vicky, Rachel, Adam, Sarah, Sam, Anne-Marie and Hannah, who walk the tough and amazing journey of faith with us.

Thank you

To Kate and the brilliant IVP guys for their support and free sandwiches.

To the team at the London Institute for Contemporary Christianity for helping us wrestle with the challenge of following Jesus in every area of our lives.

To the Romance Academy girls, Andrea and Ruth, for endless encouragement and awesome Monday morning prayer times.

To the young people from St Luke's Gamston and West Bridgford, King's Church Penwortham, Garstang Free Methodist and Fulwood Free Methodist for letting us try out *RISE* on them!

To the young disciples at Ignite who constantly inspire us with their dedication to Jesus.

Meet the authors

I (Rachel) was born in the seaside town of Weston-super-Mare but I haven't been back there since because of an unfortunate incident on the pier with an Alsatian and an ice cream cone. There were a lot of tears.

Things progressed nicely until my teenage years, when I had to tangle with spots, braces and an unfortunate tendency to dress in bizarre eighteenth-century clothing – something to do with an obsession for all things *Pride and Prejudice*.

When I found out that no one would pay me to dress like an extra in *Wuthering Heights*, I decided to take a job as a youth worker in Eastbourne. Here I spent my time setting up brilliant clubs for teenage girls and working in local schools teaching sex education.

This set me up nicely for a move to the bright lights of London, after marrying the Ginger One – more about him soon. Not content to continue with schools work which included yet more sex education, I decided to go on the telly to do a great show called *No Sex Please, We're Teenagers* – a bit of an experiment to see if a group of twelve young people would resist sexual activity for a few months so they could chat about what makes great relationships.

This led to something called the Romance Academy, which is, unsurprisingly, the name of the charity that I now head up.

Fortunately I no longer wear dodgy outfits from yesteryear, which is a good job as I travel round the country talking to cool teenagers and even cooler youth workers about sex and relationships.

I (Jason) wasn't born in a seaside town but my mum *was* born in Blackpool. I was born just up the road in Lancaster, the youngest of seven children. In the seventies, I had to share a house with five brothers, one sister, two parents, one cousin, my gran, a woolly lamb, a poodle, a labrador and the odd rabbit. I also seem to remember that there was a nine-foot orang-utan named Pickles, but disturbingly no one else in my family can recall this.

In my teenage years I didn't have too many spots, but I did have long, greasy hair and I wore a lot of black. I went on to study English and then theology in London, which is where I met the lovely Rachel.

For ten years I have been chatting, writing and speaking about how the church disciples young people for a great team of people at the London Institute for Contemporary Christianity.

And together we have worked at youth drop-ins, drop outs, weekend retreats and conferences such as Spring Harvest, Summer Madness and Soul Survivor. We love being with young people and travelling with them as we uncover just how radical, challenging and wonderful it is to follow Jesus Christ.

A lot has gone into writing this book: umpteen hundred cups of coffee, four and a half jam doughnuts, a two-day-old pizza and the odd fingernail clipping. Don't worry, IVP cleaned it all off before it got to you.

We really hope that you get as much out of this book as we have put into it – not the coffee and nail clippings, but a heartfelt desire to help all followers of Jesus Christ everywhere to love him more and more with every passing day.

Or as Paul put it,

> Peace to the brothers and sisters, and love with faith from God the Father and the Lord Jesus Christ. Grace to all who love our Lord Jesus Christ with an undying love.
>
> (Ephesians 6:23–24)

I count it a massive privilege
to be able to commend *RISE* to you.

Jason and Rachel are writing from years of
experience of loving young people into the
kingdom of God. They have always struck me as
one of those rare couples who live life so fully and
wholeheartedly that they win souls just by being themselves.
They are a couple who are going for it, living out the commands
and the substance of the kingdom of God, rather than just criticizing
the world around them. To meet them is to be challenged, encouraged
and uplifted.

The timing of this book is just right. As many of us paddle in the shallows
of what God has for us, *RISE* invites us to throw ourselves into his kingdom
head first. Often we have a desire to do this but aren't sure what it looks
like. The everyday life of a Christian can be both tough and confusing, and
sometimes it can be hard to know which is the right direction to take. What
is life really meant to be about? How do we keep going when we've messed
it up? How can we make the most of this one shot we have?

Some books treat their readers as if they are all exactly the same. This isn't
one of them. This is a book that will help you as an individual; it will relate
to who you are and your situation. It gives utterly brilliant advice about

living for Jesus while asking us all the right questions. *RISE* doesn't just tell us to 'do this or that', it helps us discover our strengths and weaknesses and how we can move forward. Anyone who engages with it cannot fail to come away with a deep sense of God speaking to them personally. If you're looking for a bridge that will connect Jesus' words to your life, or you're a youth leader looking for a new journey to take the youth group on, I can't commend this book highly enough.

Have you ever waded into a cold swimming pool? Normally we suck in our breath and let out a small scream when the water hits waist height. The half-in half-out bit is the worst. I've noticed that all of us, no matter how long we've been following God, have areas in our lives where we're half in, half out. *RISE* is all about entering fully into what Jesus has saved us for. He's called us to a destiny, a purpose, a passion, a goal, an adventure.

A while ago a survey was done in old people's care homes. It asked the question, 'What's your biggest regret in life?' Nine out of ten elderly people responded that their biggest regret wasn't a mistake they'd made; it was all the things they'd never done when they had the chance. We have that chance, we have that opportunity, it lies before us. Jesus has commanded us to live for him. We each want to meet that challenge. *RISE* is an invaluable aid to doing so.

Andy Croft
Associate Director, Soul Survivor

I was seventeen years old, with not
much faith in my life. Then it happened!
I had heard it all before, but that night this guy
told the story of Jesus, the cross, the coming back to
life, and suddenly it made sense. Deep down I just knew
it was true, and because it was true everything had to change.
Steve Clifford (Evangelical Alliance)

Think: RISE.

Think: being awake.

Think of looking at everything in your life from a different point of view.

Think of all the questions you want to ask.

Think about whether you're sure you really want the answers.

Think: 'If I know this, can I go back to things the way they used to be?'

Think: 'Do I know what I want? What am I prepared to pay for all that I want?'

Think: rise to the challenge of being a disciple of Jesus and never look back.

The search is on

Imagine you're walking down the street, when suddenly, in a blaze of blue flashing lights, four police cars turn up blocking off the ends of the road. Next the army arrive. Soldiers file out of an armoured truck, form a line and start walking up the street, looking intently at the ground. Then there's a loud whirring sound above you as helicopters appear overhead.

In the middle of all this, a policeman is looking after a woman who's looking bewildered and upset. You think to yourself, 'They're clearly looking for something, but what?'

You ask a soldier nearby, who says,

'You see that woman there?' You nod.

'Well, this morning she lost a fifty-pence piece on *this* street and *we're* going to help her find it!'

That's nuts.

Crazy. Ridiculous. No one would get in touch with the police over losing fifty pence, let alone expect to call out the army. What's fifty pence going to buy you? A pint of milk? Three-quarters of a chocolate bar? Two eighths of a DVD?

If you saw that many people searching for something, you'd rightly think that the 'something' was worth an awful lot more than fifty pence. No one searches for something that's not worth looking for.

Jesus came to look for you because you are worth finding; you are worth rescuing.

And the bigger the search party, the greater the value of the thing that's lost. God didn't leave the job of finding you up to anyone else, not even his most mighty angels. God himself came looking for you.

We sometimes think we are the ones who find God, but that's rarely the case. God used other people to reach out to you. It could have been a friend or your family. God will use every way available to him.

God found you. Which means that once you were lost.

Lost cause?

When was the last time you weren't *actually* lost but *felt* lost? Remember those times when you were a child and you were in the supermarket with your mum. Then suddenly you think 'toy aisle' and you just start wandering to find it. When you get there you start playing, but something doesn't feel right. Suddenly you realize your mum's not with you. You know where you are, but you *feel* lost – scared and worried.

Then your mum spots you, runs over and tells you off for making *her* so scared.

The Bible tells us that without God we are lost.

In Luke 15, Jesus tells stories about people who lose something precious to them – and then he describes the immense joy they feel in finding it again.

> Then Jesus told them this parable: 'Suppose one of you has a hundred sheep and loses one of them. Doesn't he leave the ninety-nine in the open country and go after the lost sheep until he finds it? And when he finds it, he joyfully puts it on his shoulders and goes home. Then he calls his friends and neighbours together and says, "Rejoice with me; I have found my lost sheep." I tell you that in the same way there will be more rejoicing in heaven over one sinner who repents than over ninety-nine righteous persons who do not need to repent.
>
> (Luke 15:3–7)

Jesus feels like that shepherd when he finds us.

He knows that when we're separated from him our lives will be filled with worry and fear, because we were never supposed to live this life alone. We were never meant to be trapped in sin that separates us from God.

> But God demonstrates his own love for us in this: while we were still sinners, Christ died for us.
>
> (Romans 5:8)

Most of the time we go about our everyday lives quite happily. We don't always feel scared and worried; we might not even realize that we are lost, but the reality – just like in the supermarket – is that we do need to be found.

It's as if we are wandering this planet without any solid idea of who we are and what we should be living for. None of us likes feeling lost, so we find lots of ways to give our lives meaning: we work hard, play hard, party hard – but at the end of the day we know that something very important is missing from our lives.

And this emptiness, this 'lost-ness', affects us all.

You don't need to be a genius to realize that as human beings we do a good job of hurting one another on a regular basis. Probably not a day goes by when we don't mess things up with a friend, argue with someone in the family, or try to get our own way, even if it means being unkind to someone else in the process. But it doesn't stop there. We turn on the news and hear about a war in some distant part of the world. Or at school we learn that in our country the rich get richer and the poor get poorer.

Something is seriously wrong with our world.

Why? Because something is seriously wrong with all of us.

We realize that the hypocrisy and greed we hate seeing all around us is also present in the way we behave. And the most frightening thing of all is that we don't seem to be able to change ourselves – it's like we have a sickness that we can't cure.

What are our options?

We can spend our entire lives trying to sort out ourselves and the rest of the world on our own. We can invent more rules and laws to try to stop people being selfish. We can name and shame everyone who says and does bad stuff. But in the end we know this is all doomed to fail.

Or we can get help from the only person who can change us and our world at the very core.

This is God's area of expertise, because what our world needs is love. John, one of Jesus' disciples, wrote in a letter to suffering Christians that no one knows love like God does.

> We know and rely on the love God has for us. God is love. Whoever lives in love lives in God, and God in them.
>
> (1 John 4:16)

Because God loved us so much he sent his Son to show us how to love; he sent his Son to *find* us. The Bible uses another expression for God 'finding' us: it talks about 'being saved'. When a goalie makes a great 'save' it means they've stopped something really bad happening to the team – a goal being scored against them.

We know that the ultimate thing that Jesus saves us *from* is a life without God. On one level you might think that life without God can't be all that bad. The sun still shines, the shops still open, the TV still works! But take a moment to think about how all the things in life have come to exist and what would happen if the being who holds everything together were to leave.

For Paul this is pretty much unthinkable. This is what he writes about Jesus to the new church in Colossae:

> He is before all things, and in him all things hold together.
>
> (Colossians 1:17)

Life without God doesn't simply mean you and me not going to church or Christian festivals any more – it means choosing to live in a world where we think that *everyone* is better off without the Creator of life, love, peace, joy, freedom. The Bible has a word for that kind of place – 'hell'. And none of us was ever meant to experience it.

Many people *do* think that life can be lived without God, that life is *better* without God. And there are others who think that the *only* option is to live without God, because they don't believe he exists in the first place.

What do you think?

The truth that Christians live by is that the *best* life possible is one that is lived in the presence of God – a life that is up close and personal with the beautiful Creator who made everything. Becoming a Christian isn't just about being saved *from* something, but *for* something. The moment we say 'yes' to Jesus, we start out on the greatest adventure of our lives and we discover something utterly priceless: a life lived side by side with God for ever.

Think about that.

And here's the strange thing. You don't have to work hard to get Jesus to give you this kind of life: everything that God gives us in Christ is free, but you do need to devote your life to uncovering just how valuable this life is. The more you give yourself to following Jesus, the more you will experience the sheer power of living in his presence every day of your life, and the more you will understand who you are and what your life is all about.

Batman versus Spider-Man

A wise old teacher once said that this is a bit like two types of superhero. First there's Batman, but everybody knows that Batman isn't really a superhero: he's a brilliant detective and a genius fighter, but all his strength and skill were gained through sheer hard work.

Then there's Spider-Man. Peter Parker doesn't *earn* his powers; he just receives them from a friendly radioactive (or genetically modified, if you've only seen the film!) spider. The story doesn't stop there though. Parker has to work out what it means to have super powers and what it means to be a hero. As his Uncle Ben tells him:

> With great power comes great responsibility.

And that goes for you too. You didn't *earn* eternal life; God decided to give you eternal life although it cost him dearly. But now that you have received it, you have to unpack what it means. You have to deal responsibly with the gift God has given you in Christ.

That doesn't mean you should try walking up a wall any time soon or start dishing out pain to the local criminals. The power that God gives you is different from that, and so much better. God gives you the power to love.

In the end, what makes life worth living is love. God says that he has an abundant supply of love that you can experience in increasing amounts. But it doesn't stop there – he also trusts you with the greatest task in the universe: passing his love on to those around you.

A heart-shaped fire

Everything that God does is motivated by love.

That's why he searched so hard for you.
Love.
The reason he made you in the first place?
Love.
God put all his heart, soul and strength into creating you.

Remember those films where you see a sword being crafted by a sword-smith in a really hot fire? Well you were made in the fire that is the father heart of God, and the only place to find life is in God.

That's why the first rule of Christianity is 'Love the LORD your God with all your heart and with all your soul and with all your strength' (Deuteronomy 6:5). God didn't give us this rule simply because he wanted our worship and adoration, though it is *so* right to give God worship and adoration. He gave us this rule because he wants us to grow and flourish (we love the word 'flourish' – it means to *really* grow, to thrive, to be successful). We do this only when we are in a relationship with him.

So, as you start reading this book, why not do this first: make your life's aim to RISE to the challenge of loving God with all your heart, all your soul and all your strength. This book will help you to realize exactly *why* you should make that your sole goal. It'll take you on a journey deeper into God's heart, as well as helping you uncover just how valuable God's gift of salvation is.

RISE

Within these pages is an invitation to live life how it's supposed to be lived as a follower of Jesus. He will make the greatest demands on you, as he asks you to give up everything you are in order to become everything he wants you to be.

Sound scary? Sure.

Is it possible? Without a doubt.

Will it be worth it? That's for you to weigh up!

Can you RISE to that?

Scattered throughout each chapter you will discover **THE WRESTLE**, a section designed to help you reflect on what you're reading.

And in case you're reading this with friends or a youth group, there is a section at the end of each chapter called **THINK TANK** with some questions to get your discussions going.

So what are you waiting for? Turn the page!

*When I was younger, life was tough
for a while. I didn't feel I could trust anyone.
I felt Jesus invited me to trust him and to know
that he wouldn't let me down. I felt God reassure
me that he had a plan for me, at a time when I didn't
even understand what the purpose of me being alive was
and at a time when I didn't even expect much for my life.*
Esther Davenport (Soul Survivor and Girl About)

I'm not saying that I have this all together, that I have it made. But I am well on my way, reaching out for Christ, who has so wondrously reached out for me. Friends, don't get me wrong: By no means do I count myself an expert in all of this, but I've got my eye on the goal, where God is beckoning us onward – to Jesus. I'm off and running, and I'm not turning back.

(Philippians 3:12–14, *The Message*)

Bring out the zombies

Have you ever had a goal in life? Could be a small goal like, 'I want the latest, greatest video game console, please!' Or a bigger goal like, 'I want to get fit', 'I want to play the violin', 'I want to own my own car', 'I want to marry the girl/boy of my dreams', 'I want to buy the Isle of Man and turn it into a lion reserve!'

If you think about it long enough, most of those goals, in one way or another, are about trying to make *you* happy (because clearly filling one of Britain's favourite isles with fur and fangs isn't going to make *everyone* happy!). Achieving any of these goals would be something that you imagine would really improve your situation *and* your enjoyment of life.

The motivation behind most of our decisions in life revolves around that one question: 'What will make me happy?' Happiness is the goal and, as most of us aren't prepared to wait around for happiness, we base our decisions on what will make us happy *now*, not later.

As part of an experiment, a group of children were given a choice: they could eat one doughnut now or they could wait for twenty minutes and then have five doughnuts. What do you think most of them chose? You got it: they went for what would make them happy now – one doughnut. They missed out on having more because they weren't prepared to wait.

But what if your goal in life isn't happiness? What if it is simply survival?

Imagine you're at a youth group meeting in the local church, when one of your friends bursts in and screams, 'Arrrggghhh! People are trying to eat me alive out there. It's a full-scale zombie apocalypse!' (In other words it's an event that brings about the end of the world.) 'Yeah right!' you say scornfully. But then you see the tear marks on his brand-new coat. You rush to a window and sure enough it's mayhem on the streets. People are being chomped on everywhere and there's a big crowd of the living dead heading towards the church.

Up to now your goal was to have a good time with mates, but things have clearly changed. Your goal now is for you and your group of friends to survive the current plague of zombies. So if you had to choose one of the following options, which one would it be?

1. Get out a notebook and pen, and brainstorm everything you know about zombies.
2. Start trying to find ways of armouring your body so that you can't be bitten.
3. Run back to your street to make sure your family and friends are OK.
4. Find ways to barricade the windows and doors of the church to seal yourselves in.

So which one did you go for? Here's the outcome of all the options:

OPTION 1: While you are brainstorming everything you know about zombies and colour coordinating your answers, the Plague of the Undead comes in through the open door and eats you.

OPTION 2: You and your friends can only find tea towels and tinfoil to help you make zombie-proof armour, so the Plague of the Undead comes in through the open door and eats you.

OPTION 3: You all split up and head for home to protect your families, only to find that they have already been bitten and are now joining the zombies who are chasing you! Guess what? The Plague of the Undead eats you.

OPTION 4: You find plenty of wood to barricade the doors, but you can't find nails or a hammer anywhere! So the Plague of the Undead comes right in through the open door and, wait for it, they eat you.

Goals and plans

Whenever human beings find themselves in a crisis, they automatically focus all their energies on what they think will help them survive. The plans we come up with are based on what we think is the best way of accomplishing that survival goal.

This is what you did with the zombie crisis. All of the above options had real benefits, but they all let you and your friends down in the end. You see, it's possible to have a good goal, but make the wrong kind of plan.

So whether your goal in life is ultimately about survival (generally most people in poorer developing countries) or happiness (generally most people in the rich West), it is essential to have a clear plan of action that will help you reach that goal.

Whatever our goal in life is, it is almost meaningless without a good plan to help us achieve it. Even the fantastic goal of becoming more like Jesus needs a plan to make it happen.

Life on Mars

We make plans all the time. It might be a plan of how to get someone to notice us, or make sure we do all our revision for exams. Whenever you set out on a journey, you have some kind of plan of how you are going to get there: which bus, which train, which motorway?

So – journey with us on this one – what if you felt that your long-term goal in life was to plant the first human colony on Mars? What do you think you'd need to do in order to achieve that goal? What would the plan look like? What kind of education would you need? How much money? How would you get the money? How hard would you have to work?

There's a real guy whose dream *is* to plant a colony on Mars. The guy's name (get ready for it) is Elon Musk.

It's a pretty extraordinary goal that requires a pretty extraordinary plan. What does it take for someone to be able to think they could accomplish that kind of goal?

Well, at the age of six he was reading for four or five hours a day.

At ten he bought his first computer and taught himself how to program it.

At ten he was also reading eight to ten hours a day.

At twelve he sold his first piece of software – a video game – for $500.

At twenty-four he sold his first media-software company for $307 million and dropped out of a course at a top American university.

He then started an online banking system called X.com. It became PayPal and he sold it to eBay in 2002 for $1.5 billion.

In 2002 he celebrated his thirtieth birthday and created Space Exploration Technologies, whose long-term goal was a mission to Mars.

In 2008 his company did what a lot of people said couldn't be done. Previously only companies funded by national governments launched space rockets. But his privately funded company launched (on the fourth attempt) Falcon 1, a rocket built for $100 million by a company with fewer than 150 employees.

If anyone's going to get humans on Mars it's Elon Musk, because this guy has had a serious approach to life. He had a big goal – so he needed a big plan.

But in case you're feeling that we are making too much of all this big goal/big plan stuff, don't worry. None of us has to be a rocket scientist at the age of six to achieve a great goal in life. And no matter how amazing the goal of a colony on Mars, Jesus has an even greater goal and plan for your life.

Right goal, wrong goal?

Below are five 'big' goals. They're not specific goals like 'being a dad by the time I'm thirty' or 'winning a gold medal at the Olympics'. They're based around the three categories that people's 'goals' in life tend to fall into – survival, happiness and success:

- Survival for themselves.
- Survival for others.
- Success for themselves.
- Success for others.

- Happiness for themselves.
- Happiness for others.

Look at the following goals and decide which category they fall into. For example, if someone buys a lottery ticket, is that about survival, success or the happiness of others?

1. A man wants to complete a list of '100 things to do before you die'. The list includes: surfing in the nude at night in Australia; running with bulls in a festival in Spain; and standing at the South Pole and having his own poo rolled away by dung beetles.
2. A woman carries a container of water a distance of six kilometres back to her village. The container weighs twenty kg – the maximum allowance of a suitcase on most air flights.
3. A thirty-three-year-old man is out surfing with his thirteen-year-old cousin when a shark attacks. The man punches the shark in the nose.
4. An eighteen-year-old girl decides to use her birthday money to get breast implants.
5. After going through four divorces, a man says that he would give up all his money for one lasting marriage.

How do you feel about these goals? What are your reactions to the people who have made these their goals in life (even if they are short-term goals)? Are the personal happiness goals (surfing nude in Australia and having a breast implant) of equal importance to the goals of survival (fetching water for the village, punching a shark to stop it attacking a young person)?

Are some goals better than others?

 # THE WRESTLE

Try to write down in a sentence what you think the goal of your life is right now.

_____

_____

Now write down what you think God's goal for your life is.

_____

_____

How similar or different are these two goals?

_____

_____

To help you achieve your goal, think of a few things you would like to commit yourself to doing as part of your plan:

1. I plan to _____

2. I plan to _____

3. I plan to _____

Think who you could chat this through with to make sure that your goal and plan in life are good and possible to achieve (with work!)

Right goal, wrong plan

Sometimes we have what we think is a good goal, but we go about achieving that goal in the wrong way.

You might have already guessed that the list of life goals you read earlier are all from real situations.

Looking back at a life of broken relationships, one man really did say that he wished one of his life goals had been to have a lasting marriage. He realized that success was a happy relationship and was even prepared to give up all his cash just to have one (and he wasn't talking about a few thousand pounds here). The man was J. Paul Getty and at the time he was one of the richest men in the world. On his deathbed he said, 'I'd gladly give up all my millions for one experience of marital happiness.'

This is the same man who had previously said, 'Who ever said money can't buy happiness didn't know where to shop.'

When he was young, his goal in life was personal success and happiness, so his plan had been to devote his life to making more and more money. He achieved the success; he could buy anything he wanted: cars, hotels, yachts. He could even buy sex if he wanted.

But his goal of personal happiness wasn't fully achieved. There was nothing wrong with him wanting to make a success of his life and be happy. We could say that he had the right goal (fulfilment), but he had the wrong plan (financial success). Money never brings the happiness that we think will fulfil us – not the lasting kind.

Sometimes your goal in life might be a good one, but the way you go about achieving it means you're never going to see it realized. Like the goal to become a world-class genius at something.

There was a big research project that aimed to find out what it takes to become really, really good at something, not just good enough to impress your friends and family, but to become an expert of the Mozart or Stephen Hawking kind.

What do you think it takes to become a genius at something? Lots of people think it's all about talent: being naturally good at something. They might say that if you're good at something it's because you were born good at it. Like professional footballers or athletes.

Other people think that this is the wrong way to look at talent. They would say that natural ability is a good start, but it doesn't amount to anything without hard work. If you are willing to put in the hard work then you can achieve anything. Like disabled athletes or mountain climbers. Thomas Edison, the inventor of the light bulb, once said, 'Genius is one percent inspiration [having a great idea] and ninety-nine percent perspiration [working hard to make that idea a reality].'

And that was the conclusion of the research: natural talent is a myth. Whatever your talent, what matters most is how much you work at it.

The research even came up with a magic number. If you want to move from becoming just good at something to being a genius, then there's a figure you need to achieve:

10,000.

That's 10,000 hours of practice. Roughly three hours a day for ten years.

So if you've got a goal in life, are you putting in the work to achieve it? Are you putting in the *right* work to achieve it? Or are you just slouching on the sofa, waiting for life to come to you?

If you want to be a great business person and you're spending five hours a day watching TV and playing video games, don't be surprised if at the end of ten years you haven't got your own business – even if you are the best gamer you know!

If you want to be a famous musician but end up online most days instead of writing songs, don't be surprised if at the end of the ten years you haven't been signed up – even if you have loads of online mates!

It matters what we spend our time doing. If you want to know what is important to someone (or where their heart is), then all you need to do is look at how they spend their time and money.

What about the goal of knowing Jesus more? If people were to take a look at your life, would they recognize that this is your goal? It's a great goal, but if your plan is just to pop along to church or youth group when you feel like it and never read your Bible or learn to listen to God for yourself, then are you really going to accomplish your goal of getting to know him better? You probably need to ask yourself whether you are really serious about following Jesus. It sounds pretty tough, doesn't it, but it's a fact that there are Christians who claim to follow Jesus, and yet they don't actually have anything in their life to show that this is what they are about. God isn't angry about this, but he is sad that they are missing out on so much.

Right goal, plan works short term, but not long term

Sometimes you have a goal and your plan works for a while, but eventually it lets you down.

Take the goal of survival – we all need to eat to stay alive. But what if your plan to survive is that you only eat food that you like, and you happen to like only fast food. In the short term the food tastes great, and it gets rid of your hunger – mission accomplished. But in the long term it leads to serious disease because your body doesn't need just *any* food, it needs the right kind of food. You might not *want* to eat five portions of fruit and vegetables a day, but to stay healthy and fit you *need* to.

Or what if your goal is happiness? Dabbling in illegal drugs may give you a happy high in the short term, but in the long run drugs bring a lot of misery through poor health, paranoia and broken relationships.

Christians aren't immune from having a fast-food, short-term approach to life. Take sex as an example.

Let's get real about the fact that as Christians we struggle with relationships and sex just as much as our friends who don't know Jesus. The difference is we know that to God sex is *so* special that it is his plan that we experience the beauty and power of it with the person we are married to. This gives us a difficult goal to aim for – but it's also a good goal. However, we shouldn't make the mistake of thinking that God is disappointed with us when we struggle, or that he doesn't want to help us. He is concerned with every area of our lives and wants to help us understand and exercise self-control in all of it: self-image, masturbation, drinking alcohol, school work, prayer, sexual curiosity, how we spend our money, family life, and so on.

In handling our guilt at messing up in these areas, we often set ourselves strict, short-term fixes that we think will make God like us again. So, if we have sex with someone, we might say we will never go out with anyone ever again; or if we can't control looking at naked images, we might want to throw away every electrical device in the house!

These might sound like good plans to help you reach the goal of being surrendered to Jesus, but they won't last long. And soon you'll find yourself back in the same old situation with a new partner or laptop.

Right goal – plan works in the short term, but doesn't last long.

Jesus' plan is for you to be set free from addiction, obsession and believing the lies that you might hear about sex and relationships. Don't get trapped into thinking that you have to sort yourself out before God will want to love and use you.

Right goal, right plan, but dreams don't always come true

Some people have a goal and a plan that *is* long term, but things still don't work out the way they had hoped.

Seventy per cent of adults in the UK play the lottery every week. Their goal is to get rich quick and their plan is to take a gamble with a one in 14 million chance of succeeding. In fact they actually have a higher chance of being hit by lightning! They have a goal (financial success) and a plan (play the lottery every week) but the odds are still stacked against them.

Another goal could be to become unbelievably famous. Someone might put in the work and practise dancing for three hours a day for ten years, but their dream still doesn't come true because so many people are trying to be famous. The odds against them becoming famous are increasing all the time.

Remember the guy who made a list of '100 things to do before you die?' That sounded like a good plan for happiness, but that man died at the age of forty-seven, before he'd completed half of his list!

We will all face circumstances in life that we can't control. There might be times when we do everything 'right' (we're diligent at college, work hard at our talent, fill in every application form going) and still not achieve our dream. *X Factor* feeds off people's broken dreams and most of us know how that feels. You might have come across an older Christian who had the 'right' plan in life: they read their Bible, didn't have sex, lived for others and so forth, yet their dreams of getting married, landing their dream job or having children didn't come true. Obviously this is a really painful reality for some people, but those who choose to make knowing Jesus their goal still find joy and fulfilment – why? Because in Jesus they have found life in all its fullness.

If our goal is to know Jesus better, we are given a better dream for our lives – one that is attainable because he is investing in it too. Do you know what his ambition is for you? That you live life to the full. It's his dream that you grow in love and service of God and, by doing so, become a world-changer. You might do this as an artist, a businessperson, a scientist or a youth worker . . . but it's the same dream and we *can* reach it.

Right goal, right plan, no buts

OK, so we have talked about:

a) having the right goal in life;
b) having the right goal but making the wrong kind of plan to get there;
c) having the right goal *and* the right plan, but things still don't work out the way we'd hoped.

So now you are probably asking:

Is it possible to have the right goal *and* the right plan that *works*? In other words, is it possible to be happy and fulfilled in this life?

Well, let's ask you a question in response. If your goal in life is knowing Jesus and your plan is following him, will this help you live a truly joy-filled and fulfilling life? You know what's supposed to be the right answer but do you really believe it? Do you act as if you believe it?

When Jesus says, 'I have come that [you] may have life, and have it to the full' (John 10:10) he means it! Jesus' goal is for you to experience the best life possible. The great and mysterious thing is that a relationship with Jesus is both the *right goal* and the *right plan*.

Jesus is the perfect expression of the best life possible. You can't separate the two: Jesus is life and life to the full. He is the goal and he is the plan – and it works! Not in a magic kind of way, but it makes the best sense, doesn't it?

Gold trainers

Let's say you really, really wanted to buy a pair of gold trainers – not just gold in colour but actually made of real gold. We don't know why you'd want such a pair – you couldn't run in them and you'd struggle to pick them up, but let's just say that you do. Now there's only one shop in the entire world that stocks them. But the weird thing is, they don't sell them, they give them away for free. Now imagine that although you spend your whole life going around saying, 'I want a pair of gold trainers, I sooo want a pair of gold trainers', you never visit the shop. Guess what? You're not going to get hold of the shiny, heavy footwear.

Jesus is very clear that when it comes to life and life to the full there's only one person to go to. That's not going to change, ever. You might seek out fulfilment and joy in life without going to Jesus, but the fact is that you're not going to find it.

So your relationship with Jesus is the goal *and* it is the plan. It is the goal that every other dream and ambition of your life must fall in line with, and it becomes your benchmark against which to judge the choices you have to make.

Q. Should I spend a week with mates in Costa-del-blotto, off my face on alcohol every night?
A. Does it fit in line with my goal of becoming more like Jesus in my character and actions?

Q. Is this university course in graphic design the right one for me?
A. Does it fit in with my goal of using my natural skills and talents to serve Jesus and be a blessing to the world?

Q. Should I go out with that cute guy/girl who is great but doesn't share my love of Jesus?
A. Will he/she help me grow in my dedication to following Jesus with my whole life?

Have you got the right goal? Have you got the right plan?

Your journey of knowing Jesus as life and inviting him to help you live it to the full is completely dependent on your plan to follow him. The biggest question you need to ask yourself is whether your plan for your life and what you are doing now are helping or frustrating your journey towards that goal.

And if you know you're making choices that aren't directed towards this goal, then the chances are you're not completely convinced that following Jesus is the perfect plan for happiness. Don't worry, part of the journey of this book is to help you put your trust one hundred per cent in God's plan.

● THINK TANK

Take a moment and ask yourself how serious you are about knowing Jesus better. If your answer is, 'Yes, I am a follower of Jesus and I want to get serious about knowing him better', then now is the moment to ask Jesus to help you form a new plan to grow in your relationship with him. It will involve finding ways to get into God's Word (Bible-reading notes, podcasts of talks, Bible-in-a-year schemes, etc.) and chatting with God more (on your own and with friends). It will also mean finding wiser Christians you can ask all sorts of questions.

Why not make a quick note of the things that are going to be in your new plan to help you grow in your relationship with Jesus.

1. _____

2. _____

3. _____

Discussion starters

• Do you think all our actions fall into one of these categories?
   Survival for ourselves
   Survival for others
   Success for ourselves
   Success for others
   Happiness for ourselves
   Happiness for others

- For many people, love is the goal in life, as one song says, 'The greatest thing you'll ever learn is how to love and be loved in return.'[1] Do you think that's true?
- What are some of the short-term ways we have of finding love? Do they work in the long term?
- Is everything else a substitute for love? Money, fame, sex – is it all just fast food? Does it really give us what we need in the end?
- How can you support one another in achieving your goals, especially the one about knowing Jesus better?

*I think there comes a point in life
where you have to try to answer life's
questions for yourself. You can no longer
ride the faith of your family and friends. When
I was sixteen years old I had to stand back and ask
myself, 'Do I believe in everything I have been told about
Jesus and truth?' It's a scary thing to do. To really question and
examine your faith. I think this is why Jesus said to his disciples
'Who do you say that I am?' He was inviting them on a journey to
find out who he was. This is the greatest journey I have been on in
my life . . . and I'm still asking questions and finding my way.*
Kevin McGlade (29th Chapter)

God's wisdom is something mysterious that goes deep into the
interior of his purposes. You don't find it lying around on the surface.
It's not the latest message, but more like the oldest – what God
determined as the way to bring out his best in us, long before we
ever arrived on the scene. The experts of our day haven't a clue
about what this eternal plan is. If they had, they wouldn't have killed
the Master of the God-designed life on a cross. That's why we have
this Scripture text:

No one's ever seen or heard anything like this,
Never so much as imagined anything quite like it –

What God has arranged for those who love him.
But you've seen and heard it because God by his Spirit has
brought it all out into the open before you.
(1 Corinthians 2:9–10, *The Message*)

Ain't no mountain high enough

Imagine that you and four friends are walking through the middle of a jungle. Why? Because someone has told you there is a mysterious mountain in the middle of this jungle, and at the top of the mountain there is a funky coffee shop. Well, perhaps it's something a little bit better than that: maybe it's a wise old woman who knows the answer to every question ever asked, someone for whom *nothing* is a mystery.

So you and your friends eventually break free from the undergrowth and trees and step into a clearing. Not just any clearing either, because rising into the clear sky above you is the mountain. You can just about make out a little fire at the top, and you think, 'That must be the cave of the wise woman!'

The problem is that there are five paths up the mountain. Five paths that head upwards. Now all five of them could take you to the top, or just one of them might, or all five could lead you astray. As individuals you could each take a path, but how will you let one another know whether or not your path is the right one? And no, you don't have GPS *or* phone coverage!

We'll come back to the mysterious mountain at the end of the chapter.

A good detective

Have you noticed how addictive a good mystery is? We love a story that starts with an unsolved crime that slowly unravels over time. Be it *Scooby Doo*, *CSI* or *Sherlock Holmes*, mysteries keep us hooked.

But even the stories that aren't outright mysteries do contain mysteries. Most plots involve suspense, and even the best period dramas or chick flicks will keep you wondering: will she dump that scoundrel and find true love with the dependable bloke who's a bit quiet but will see her right? Will Mr Right realize that love is not about money, cars and girls, but about honesty, commitment and faithfulness?

Have you ever thought about *your* life as a mystery? We're not saying that during your few years on earth you've managed to gain an arch enemy who's thwarting your goals at every turn and your job is to suss out what they're up to next. Nor is it, necessarily, that you're part of a gang who solve local mysteries like 'who ate all the pies?' on a regular basis.

But a huge part of life is about unlocking mysteries: why are you here? What will you do with your life?

To a toddler all the sounds that come out of an adult's mouth must be an absolute mystery, but eventually they understand them.

For me (Jason), most of the sounds that came out of my French teacher's mouth were an utter mystery! But if you stick with it, 'unlocking' the mystery that is French can bring about lots of possibilities. You could become a

French teacher, get a job translating French, move to France and marry someone who's French and doesn't speak any English! The possibilities are endless.

Most learning begins by being faced with a mystery that we have to overcome. You might not remember as far back as this, but at one time everything we've typed so far was just squiggles and lines on a page – like a code you had to learn to decipher. Just as at one time you learnt that the strange sounds coming out of your parents' mouths actually *meant* something like 'book' or 'ball' or 'stop hitting your sister'.

So solving mysteries can help us with our learning. For example, our two nephews are faced with a *big* mystery. As they grow up they're learning not just one language, but two! Their father is British and their mother is Austrian, so their dad speaks to them in English and their mum in German.

It's hard enough learning one language, let alone two, but some genius scientists have discovered that those children who have to work at learning two languages from an early age have an increased ability to learn. The brain is a bit like any muscle in the body: the more you exercise it, the bigger the load it can take.

The big mystery

It's really amazing how many folk don't ask the big questions about life! Not many people in our country have a burning desire to find out why we exist at all. How did we get on this planet? What are we here for?

What happened to our curiosity? Working at *solving* life's mysteries is good for us.

We love 'Wodwo' by Ted Hughes. It's a poem that celebrates mystery and curiosity:

What am I? Nosing here, turning leaves over
Following a faint stain on the air to the river's edge
I enter water. Who am I to split
The glassy grain of water looking upward I see the bed
Of the river above me upside down very clear
What am I doing here in mid-air? Why do I find
this frog so interesting as I inspect its most secret
interior and make it my own? Do these weeds
know me and name me to each other have they
seen me before do I fit in their world? I seem
separate from the ground and not rooted but dropped
out of nothing casually I've no threads
fastening me to anything I can go anywhere
I seem to have been given the freedom
of this place what am I then? And picking
bits of bark off this rotten stump gives me
no pleasure and it's no use so why do I do it
me and doing that have coincided very queerly
But what shall I be called am I the first
have I an owner what shape am I what
shape am I am I huge if I go
to the end on this way past these trees and past these trees
till I get tired that's touching one wall of me

> for the moment if I sit still how everything
> stops to watch me I suppose I am the exact centre
> but there's all this what is it roots
> roots roots roots and here's the water[1]

Not many people start their day with this kind of curiosity about life, but you could do. Not by eating frogs or taking chunks out of tree stumps, but you *could* be that curious. Life presents you with a billion mysteries every day. Are you just going to let them pass you by?

For instance, how is it that you're able to speak, to form words and sentences? You think of something to say in your head and almost instantly it's coming out of your mouth. It's amazing when you stop to think about it! How do you do that? How do you *remember* what to say? How do you remember what you had for breakfast yesterday?

Being curious and seeking answers to questions has enabled humankind to make so much progress. We take a great deal for granted, but most of the stuff we use every day is a mystery to us. Your mobile phone for instance – you know how to *work* it but do you know how it *works*? We know that it's electricity and chips and stuff. Great, but if you suddenly got zapped back in time a couple of hundred years, do you think you'd be able to explain properly what a mobile phone is, let alone try to make one yourself?

'Wodwo' is a *great* poem precisely because it stops to ask, 'Who are we and why do we do what we do?'

But if that's not a question you're asking, if it's not a question most of your friends are asking, why not? And if we stop looking for answers, if we stop trying to solve mysteries, will we still advance as humankind?

THE WRESTLE

If we started each day by asking questions we couldn't answer, we might not even get out of bed. It could be a pretty good excuse: 'Sorry, Mum, can't get up today. I'm busy trying to work out how I can travel faster than light by using this rubber band and a nine-volt battery.'

But what are the 'mysteries' you're facing day by day? What are the questions you're asking? Look at the following questions and see if they connect with you in any way:

- Where am I and how did I get here?
- Am I lost or am I already home?
- When will this stop?
- How do I get confidence?
- What am I good at?
- Will you still love me tomorrow?
- Which way is up?
- Am I attractive?
- How do I get the best life now?
- Will I ever be what I want to be?
- Can you prove it?
- What will it take to get me where I want to go?

Where's the shotgun?

Video and computer games *always* present you with mysteries you need to solve in order to advance. Could be a riddle or puzzle that helps you open a magic gateway, or it could be a big search that leads you to the upgrade you need to defeat the next big alien/martial arts expert/orc. When I (Jason)was a teenager, I spent a huge amount of time asking, 'Where's the shotgun?'– meaning 'This pistol etc. isn't powerful enough to help me cut a swathe of destruction through the next onslaught of endlessly re-spawning bad guys!'

You might think that that's not an important question (and you would probably be right), but we spend many hours playing computer games, so a huge amount of our time is dedicated to answering questions like that or something similar.

The other question I was asking from that list is one that most people ask *throughout* their lives: 'How do I get confidence?'

For instance, when you're eight or nine you don't care that much what the opposite sex thinks of you. But a few years later it can often seem that that's all you care about. How do you get the confidence to ask someone out? Many is the time I started to dial a girl's number, only to stop because I became too embarrassed at the prospect of actually speaking to her! Hard to believe, but this was in the days before texting and instant messaging!

And what about getting confidence to be yourself with a group of friends? Or with a group of people you want to be your friends? So much of what we want to accomplish in our lives depends on having confidence – the boldness, the courage or the experience we need in order to overcome our fear and take a risk.

Am I attractive?

Sometimes the questions we're asking can be answered by asking another question. When you're wondering what kind of career to choose, try asking, 'What am I good at?' or 'What am I passionate about?' to help you figure out the answer to your first question.

And sometimes your question is really part of a bigger question. 'Am I attractive?' is really asking, 'Am I loved?' Most people are happy to take the substitute 'answer' – that as long as folk find them attractive, they don't really care if they're loved. But being loved and being thought of as sexy are two very different things. If someone thinks you're sexy, they are probably only seeing you as a 'sex object', but if someone loves you, they will see you as a whole person and want to get to know you better.

Out in the desert

Those are some of the questions we are asking, but are there others we haven't thought of yet? Could there be other mysteries we need to solve in order to understand life and to experience it fully?

There are some mysteries we can afford to ignore, that we can live without knowing the answer to. Like, why is the fluff in your belly button always blue? And why do people want to surf in the nude?

But then there are other mysteries that life chucks our way that we simply can't afford to ignore.

Imagine you woke up this morning and found yourself not in your bedroom but in a silky tent lying on cushions. You step outside and you're in the desert: there are camels, sand dunes and a hot, blazing sun. You'd rightly be thinking, 'Hang on, I went to bed in a terraced house in Birmingham and woke up here. What's going on?' You'd no doubt freak out slightly, particularly if you're not from Birmingham in the first place.

As it turns out you have been kidnapped. Let's say a random bandit stole into your house and decided to see how you'd like life in the middle of a desert. The guy is obviously nuts, which might influence your next action: escape by any means necessary.

But what if your kidnapper is a billionaire sheikh who tells you your life up to now has been a lie. The truth is that you were kidnapped as a baby by the people who say they're your family back in Birmingham, when in fact you're his long-lost offspring and he wants you to inherit the multi-billion-pound fortune that is rightly yours!

That will probably impact your next action. Instead of running to find the nearest friendly camel to get you back to the UK, you will settle back on the cushions and wait for the servants to attend to your every whim, before buying your very own shopping mall and Manchester United.

Having found yourself in a bizarre situation, the answer to the question 'what do I do next?' is utterly dependent on the answer to the question 'how did I get here?'

The biggest question you have to answer is always 'what do I do with my life?', but your response is completely dependent on how you answer one of the big mysteries of life:

How did I get on planet earth in the first place?

Your answer to this question, the solution to this mystery, should impact every decision you make for the rest of your life.

Why? Because this is the mystery to trump all mysteries.

When we begin to dig into that mystery we find one of two things. Either we come to the conclusion that life is purely chance, and even if our family love us and wanted to have us, our existence is a fluke. Or we discover a God who has infinite wisdom and knowledge of his entire creation and holds the answers to all the questions we will ever have. And it matters which conclusion we come to, because it affects how we answer all the smaller questions in life.

Better than knowing that our family loves us is knowing that God loves us – not just a head knowledge ('yes, I know God has to love us because he created us') but a day-by-day, deeply connected relationship with God that makes us increasingly aware of just how much the Father, the Son and the Spirit love us.

Nothing, nothing at all, and we'll say it again, nothing, will give you confidence like knowing that God loves you, God lives in you and God delights in you. You have to make the leap from understanding this in your head to knowing it as a very real truth in your everyday life.

The reality is that you are on this planet because God loves you. Let that sink in for a while: the reason you are here is because of God's love. When God decided to create you, he didn't just think you up in his head but in his heart as well.

You have a lot of questions. A lot of those questions are born out of fear, out of a lack of confidence in who you are. God's word to you is that 'perfect love drives out fear' (1 John 4:18). This means that, as you grow in your understanding of God's love for you, you will grow in confidence too, and that means your worries about being accepted, being confident, being loved will grow smaller and smaller as God's love in your heart grows bigger and bigger.

This doesn't happen instantly. Most of us have to remind ourselves time and again that God loves us, in order for it really to sink in. That won't be a short journey. Jesus will dedicate himself to the task of driving fear out of your life, but only if you work with him, not against him.

Now let's head back to that mountain.

Back to the mountain

Remember that we left you and your four friends at the foot of the mountain, wondering which of the five paths would lead you to the top? Have you got any ideas yet? You *could* all try and find the way by each taking a path, but you've not got a map or Sat Nav so your chances of finding the wise woman are slim, to say the least.

But what if the wise woman came to you? What if she walked down the mountain on the right path? You wouldn't even need to climb – all you'd have to do would be to ask and you'd have the answers to 'life, the universe, everything'!

This image has often been used as a way to illustrate the difference between Christianity and other big stories (other religions and philosophies) about the meaning of life. Some say you have to find your own path; others say we can work our own way to God; some even say that there is no 'wise woman' at the top.

But surely it makes sense that, just as only the wise woman knows the path up and down the mountain, only God knows the way to God. And God hasn't made it difficult for us to know him, because he reveals himself through his Son Jesus: God comes to us. Although God is mysterious, he still makes it easy for people to know him by his becoming one of us, by becoming human, a real person in history, and not just that, but the most *influential* person in history.

Many people, particularly in the Western world, doubt that it's so simple. They believe that the very idea of God, let alone of Jesus as God, is a lie. So in our culture the very existence of God remains a mystery, something we truly doubt. If we even doubt that God is real, how can we ever have confidence that he loves us?

Read this verse from the Bible a few times and allow the truth of God's love for you to settle in your heart and mind. Why not memorize it and remind yourself about God's love every day?

This is how God showed his love among us: he sent his one and only Son into the world that we might live through him. This is love: not that we loved God, but that he loved us and sent his Son as an atoning sacrifice for our sins.

(1 John 4:9–10)

 THINK TANK

- If you were the heir to a billionaire's fortune, what would you buy first?
- Have you ever found yourself asking questions like, 'Am I attractive?' or 'What am I good at?' What answers did you come up with? What do you think God's answers to those questions would be?
- What gives you the most confidence? Is it knowing you're talented? Knowing you're liked?
- How do we begin to know that someone loves us in *any* relationship?
- How do we begin to really understand that God loves us?

*I was under a lot of peer pressure
at school. I was being told I must have
sex to be considered 'a man', even though
I did not want to. Jesus offered a different path,
one that allowed me to be myself and be accepted.
By following him, I would, and did, find true fulfilment.*
Andre Adefope

> Go out into the world uncorrupted, a breath of fresh air in this
> squalid and polluted society. Provide people with a glimpse of good
> living and of the living God. Carry the light-giving Message into the
> night so I'll have good cause to be proud of you on the day that
> Christ returns.

> (Philippians 2:14–16, *The Message*)

The peer steer

You may be in agreement with us so far, or you may not. You might put
your hand in the air (not literally – people will stare) and say:

- 'I agree that following Jesus is both the goal and the plan for my life.
  A relationship with the God who created me is the purpose of my life.'
- 'There's a part of me that knows all the answers to the mysteries
  and questions I have can be found in Jesus.'

But there may also be a part of you that feels unsure. When it comes to life and life to the full, you are still wondering if Jesus is the key to unlocking everything.

Is Jesus really 'the way and the truth and the life' as John says (John 14:6)?

How do we decide what truth is? How do we decide what's the right and the wrong way to live our lives? How do we know that we are going the right way?

Sometimes it's about doing the detective work. We look at the science and work out that something makes good sense.

At other times we might be tempted to go with a feeling, with an intuition. How many times have you heard people say, 'This *feels* good, so it must be right'?

Often we're pretty sure that the decision we've come to is our own choice, but is that *always* the case?

A psychologist once did an experiment in school. During a normal maths lesson one of the students was sent out on a fake errand. While she was gone the psychologist explained what was going to happen: the maths teacher would do a quick test with five questions, nothing too difficult. After the test the teacher would run through the answers, asking someone for their answer first, then the rest of the class were to put their hands in the air if they had the same answer. However, they agreed that for the fourth question the student would give the *wrong* answer. The teacher would pretend that it was correct, and when he asked the class who got the same answer, they would all raise their hands again.

Of course, the student on the errand had no idea about this arrangement. So when she returned to class she took the test like everyone else.

The psychologist did this experiment in several schools. Whenever it came to the fourth question, nearly every student who'd been sent on 'an errand', even though they'd written the *right* answer on their sheet, would put their hand in the air with everybody else to say they'd put the *wrong* answer down. Although they were right, they went along with the crowd who said that the *wrong* answer was right!

Why did they do that?

It's because of something called the 'peer steer'. Sometimes we come to a conclusion on our own, but more often than not, we reach an answer because we've let others 'steer' or direct our thinking.

The odd one out

You need to remember this when thinking about your faith in Jesus.

A definition of religion or spirituality is that it's simply about 'lining yourself up with the truth of the universe'. Which basically is saying that there is a *big* Truth out there (God) that you decide to believe in, a truth that pretty much makes sense of everything.

Whether or not someone is a Christian, they will believe something about life and death (and everything in between) that makes the most sense to them. They might *not* be religious or see themselves as 'spiritual', but they live according to what they think feels right. For example, they might want to get married in a church rather than in a registry office because they like the tradition of God's blessing on their marriage – even though they don't believe it's real.

Clearly there are different conclusions in society about *what* the big truth of the universe might be.

And these different conclusions result in entire cultures 'acting' very differently from one another.

For instance, most people in Britain don't actively worship God because they've come to the conclusion that either God doesn't exist or his existence doesn't affect their everyday life. That's what they see as the truth and they believe it. It's very different from what Christians believe, and this can make things tricky for us when our school mates or our family think that they are right and we are wrong, or even nuts. It can make some Christians feel outnumbered and worried about letting people know that they follow Jesus.

It's like the large majority of people around you putting their hand in the air and saying, 'God isn't real.' Are you going to be the one person who *doesn't* put their hand in the air to say they've got it wrong and you've got it right? Not easy being the odd one out, is it? When we're surrounded by thousands of our peers all worshipping God at a Christian festival, it's easy to say the rest of our society has got it wrong. Not so easy at school, college or university, when we are in the minority.

But the thing is that if the world were a classroom, the people *not* believing in God would be the odd ones out!

Over 90% of the world's population believe in a god of some description or in the supernatural. And 5% of the rest haven't made up their mind whether God exists or not. So that leaves only 5% who are waving their hands in the air saying that God is a fairy tale.

The challenge for us is that we live among that last 5%. So in our country there's a large section of the population saying, 'The only reason you believe God exists is because all the people you've grown up with (i.e. your church) say God exists, but they're wrong!' However, you can flip that argument around to say the exact opposite: 'The only reason you believe God *doesn't* exist is because the people you've grown up with say God doesn't exist, but they're wrong!' You might even want to add, 'Look at the rest of the world. Why are 5% supposedly smarter than all the rest? If it's so obvious God isn't real why do 90% of the planet believe there *is* a God?'

Obviously evangelism isn't about Christians rolling out a few God statistics every time we feel picked on for what we believe! And not everyone on the planet believes in the same god, but the reality is that in the West, most of the time people can't even be bothered to *consider* whether there is a God – they just get on with living their life. Shouting about sin and hell on street corners isn't really going to change that.

Powerful and personal

The sad reality is that most people in our country act as if God doesn't exist. Whether or not they actually say it out loud, at some level they believe one of two things: either God doesn't exist, or if he does exist, then that force, entity, old bloke with a beard (whatever they think God is) has no desire or right to interrupt the way they live their life.

As one Christian teacher, Rob Bell, put it, they believe God to be powerful but impersonal. They say that God created everything that exists but he has no interest in entering into relationship with any part of his creation or shaping its destiny.

Christianity believes the first part of that but not the second. Which is why Christians are described as followers of Jesus. We're *following* a person: we're dedicated to a living, breathing human who also happens to be God, and we define our identity by our relationship with Jesus and with all those who are also committed to following him. We become part of God's family.

By and large people live their lives according to one of three different views:

1. God doesn't exist.
2. God exists and he's powerful but impersonal.
3. God exists and he's powerful and personal.

So how do people's actions line up with these different theories? Clearly if you believe something, you act according to that belief. As the poet T. S. Eliot once said, 'Behaviour is belief.' For example, most people totally believe in the law of gravity and act in tune with that belief. We can't 'see' gravity but we know its effects, and so we don't tend to jump out of aeroplanes unless we are attached to a parachute!

But whether you believe in gravity or not, you are affected by it – so what about something even more difficult to see, like having a belief in someone's love for you?

Knowing that you are loved can give you the confidence to take a risk, because you know that no matter what happens that person or group who loves you isn't going to stop loving you. And the more confidence you have in them loving you, the more you will act according to that confidence.

So when you look at your actions, what do they *say* you believe about God?

God is powerful . . .

The Bible says that God is ruler over the entire universe.

> Acknowledge and take to heart this day that the LORD is God in heaven above and on the earth below.
>
> (Deuteronomy 4:39)

God is totally and utterly in control. We know we can turn to him in times of immense pain and suffering because he has the power to heal and forgive. We acknowledge that he has standards for us to live up to, and we will all be judged by him on how we have lived our lives.

. . . and God is personal.

The Bible also says that we can know God through Jesus.

> Jesus answered, 'I am the way and the truth and the life. No-one comes to the Father except through me. If you really know me, you will know my Father as well. From now on, you do know him and have seen him.'
>
> (John 14:6–7)

When Jesus was on earth, people touched him and knew him as a personal friend. We also experience a personal relationship with him and talk about being touched by his intimate love and kindness.

The God we see in the Bible and get to know through Jesus is both powerful and personal.

It's hard to get our heads around this, because we tend to see powerful people as distant and impersonal (think of the President of the USA), and personal people (like our family and friends) as not powerful (they can't change the world). But this truth is totally unique to Christianity and is a really important way of understanding who God is.

To you and me, the law of America is powerful but impersonal. You recognize that it *has* power but that it has no power over you. If you are a British citizen in the UK, you can break an American law and not fear the consequences because you don't live there.

Unless, of course, it's a similar law to one we have in Britain. For you, British law is both powerful and personal. That means if you break a British law you have to face the consequences (if you get caught, that is) – the British government has power over you to do as the law decides.

But imagine you're the child of the British Prime Minister. One of the PM's chief jobs is to create and maintain our laws and to see that they are enforced for the good of all society. He has the power to enforce the law but he is also your dad! He is powerful *and* personal.

Let's say, though, that you break the law. Would breaking the law still have consequences for you, or would the 'personal' relationship you have with the Prime Minister influence whether you get into trouble or not? Let's hope not, otherwise the Prime Minister is corrupt!

And that's a bit like our relationship with our powerful and personal God, except it's *way* more amazing than having the PM for a parent! God is our parent – we pray 'Our Father . . .', but he's not going to bend the rules of the universe for us!

The perfect family

God governs the universe with laws that are designed to bring the greatest benefit for everyone. His laws are not a random bunch of rules to keep people doing what he says – they come from God's deep love for everything and everyone he has made.

One of the amazing things we learn about God is that he is three – a trinity (Father, Son and Holy Spirit). It's a mysterious idea, one of the greatest mysteries of the universe, but one of the blindingly clear truths of the cosmos is that God is family, God is community. And not just any community, but a community that is perfect in love and unity. God the Father loves the Son and the Holy Spirit and so on. And God wants everything he has made to experience this kind of love and unity, this kind of family.

When we break God's laws we don't just pay for it ourselves, we experience it in all our relationships. This is what sin is – it's the disease of selfishness. Being selfish means that we always put ourselves, and our own needs, before everyone else. This is the quickest way to break up friendships, marriages, families and countries.

We have all been on the receiving end of other people's selfishness. Some of us might have been responsible for hurting others: have you ever cheated on your boy/girlfriend? Been two-faced with your friends? Put yourself and your needs before other people's? Selfishness is like a disease that we all suffer from and so all our relationships suffer too. We can't help but pass it on and on and on . . .

When humanity thinks it can do a better job of running the universe than God can, we end up with a series of fractured relationships. So if we look at how the world is run, we often see that those in power seek to create a paradise for the few and a hell for the many. Our laws can often be biased towards keeping the powerful and rich, powerful and rich.

Most people live as if God's rules for the best life in his universe don't exist. That's mainly because they don't believe God himself exists. They're simply acting on what they understand to be the truth of the universe.

Think about some of the 'basic' truths you live by every day and how your behaviour matches those truths:

- **Truth 1:** If you don't eat, not only will you get hungry but eventually you'll die!
- **Action:** I'm going to eat.
- **Truth 2:** Singing out loud is only acceptable in some situations, for example in church, in a football stadium, on stage, in the shower.
- **Action:** Sing out loud in those situations, but not on the bus or in the middle of a maths lesson.

Now you've got the idea: what are the actions that best match the following *if* they were true:

- **Truth 1:** God does exist but doesn't care whether you exist or not. (He's powerful but impersonal.)
- **Truth 2:** God does exist and has a goal for your life that he wants to help you fulfil. (He's powerful and personal.)

There are people who go to church who believe Truth 1 (which of course isn't the complete truth), and you can tell by their actions. They pretty much do what they want most of the time and pop along to church to keep God (or their family) happy.

The Bible points us in the direction of Truth 2. God does exist and has a goal for your life that he invests in with you. It's a profound truth but also really challenging because it means that it matters how we live our lives. We can't just do what we want any more. God is in this with us and what he says goes!

But if we know this is the ultimate Truth, why don't we always *act* as if God is a real, powerful and personal presence in our lives and this universe?

To understand this more we need a little bit of a battle.

Batman versus the Joker

When it comes to understanding the origin of everything – why we're here in the first place – it's kind of like a fight between Batman and the Joker. Yep, there's Batman again.

The Joker is about chaos.

For him life in this universe is nothing but a cosmic joke, an accident; ultimately there is no reason why we're here, so *pick* a reason, any one will do.

If you believe you are here because of chaos or an accident, then the action is that you should do what you want because life is what you make it.

Then there's Batman.

For him the universe is born of order and design. The law must be obeyed and justice must be served in order to bring about the best for humankind. Otherwise we'll descend into chaos.

If you believe you are here because of order, then the action is that you choose to do what God wants because life is what God makes it. It makes sense that God, the source of all life, knows best how life should be lived.

So are you more like the Joker or Batman?

We grow up being told that to live the best life possible we must do what *we* want to do as individuals, when *we* want to do it. But the most liberating life we can lead is in serving God's law, becoming a slave to it in fact. It sounds strange to say that we find freedom in slavery, but that's exactly what Jesus said it would mean to follow him.

 **THE WRESTLE**

We often act according to what we believe about *ourselves*. For example, if we're given the opportunity to perform in front of others – could be singing, acting or giving a talk – do we say 'no' because we believe the truth is that we can't do it? Or do we act according to what we think *other people* will believe about us? We don't sing/speak/dance in front of people because we imagine everyone will think we're an idiot if we get it wrong? Which is it?

What truths about yourself do you need to start believing? What lies do you need to ask Jesus to help you debunk?

God's truth about me . . . (To help you get started, read Psalm 139:14 and Deuteronomy 7:6. Genesis 15:1 will tell you what God wants to be for you.)

_____

_____

Lies I'm not going to believe any more . . . (Is there someone you trust who could help you think of lies you don't want in your life any more? They could pray with you and help you begin to stamp on the lies and live in the truth about who you are, what you can do and all God has for you.)

_____

_____

The oldest lie in the book

We're about to dish out some gold now: a truth so valuable that it might as well have a £10 billion price tag on it. It's a nugget of wisdom so rich that:

1. We wish we'd thought of it,

and

2. We wish someone had told us about it when we first committed our lives to God.

It's a pearl of wisdom we got from Dallas Willard, a bit of a hero of ours when it comes to learning how to follow Jesus. He said:

> Being a disciple of Jesus means understanding that Jesus knows how to live your life better than you do.

Most Christians would put their hand in the air if you asked them if they believed this to be true. But remember what old T. S. Eliot said? 'Behaviour is belief.' There are many who sign up to the truth of this statement but their behaviour doesn't match up to it: belief and action aren't the same.

Most decisions in life are made without inviting Jesus to be a part of the conversation. Think about that: if we don't invite Jesus' wisdom to shape our everyday decisions, is that because we think he doesn't care?

Or is it because we know he cares too much about the choices we make and that we don't want him to interfere? We much prefer *our* choice? Or is there a third option – that we don't think Jesus will get it right?

I (Rachel) know a teenage guy at the moment who is struggling to believe in God and live for him. His biggest hurdle is whether to choose to trust God with his life. He doesn't know if God loves him enough, or if he loves God enough to hand over the control of his life.

In a way it's not surprising that this is the case. The very first relationship humans had with God broke down because of a lack of trust. God provided Adam and Eve with everything they could ever want in the Garden of Eden. But instead of realizing what a good thing they had, they were persuaded that the opposite was true and believed one of God's enemies when he said, 'God does *not* know how to live your life better than you do.'

That enemy is the devil, and if you're going to be a disciple of Christ then you need to be aware that the devil is going to make sure that you hear this lie as often as possible, in as many ways as possible, using all the finite power he possesses.

'God is holding good stuff back from you and doesn't know how to give you the best life possible.'

It's a total and utter lie.

But the devil is very successful at sowing chaos and disorder through this lie. Think about all the laws that we have, all the laws that God set up in the Old Testament. In the account of the creation in Genesis there was originally just one law. God places Adam and Eve in a paradise and gives them one simple rule to obey: 'Do not eat from the tree of the knowledge of good and evil.'

There are entire books written on what that rule really meant. But at the heart of it is God's desire to give Adam and Eve a choice – to give them free will. Ever thought, 'Why doesn't God just put that tree somewhere else out of harm's way?' It's because God wanted to say to Adam and Eve, 'Guys, do you trust me? Do you trust the fact that my life is devoted to bringing about the best possible life for you? That's why I've put you in a beautiful paradise.'

Of course, it all goes horribly wrong when humankind decides to trust the devil: that there is a better way than God's way – *our way*. We've prized our independence over believing and trusting that obeying God brings about the best life, and as a result our planet, our communities, our families and we ourselves have paid the price.

As Christians, we realize that Christ himself paid the price for the damage we caused to the universe when we lined ourselves up with the devil's rebellion against God.

Perhaps you're still in that place asking, dare I trust God? Dare I trust Jesus with my entire life? Can I trust that Jesus is who he says he is – that he *is* life and life to the full? The one rule in the Garden of Eden was an invitation to trust God wholeheartedly. And Jesus continues to make bold, bright and beautiful invitations to people that will bring about real and lasting fulfilment if they just trust in him and his words.

 **THINK TANK**

In this chapter we have talked about the many ways that followers of Jesus can be tempted to believe this lie: 'God is holding good stuff back from you and doesn't know how to give you the best life possible.'

- What do you think of the above statement?
- Have there been times when you have believed that you couldn't fully trust God with your life?
- If so, how did you handle this? What did you do to remind yourself of the fact that no one knows and loves you like God does?

Fight to the finish . . .

Paul was a fantastic follower of Jesus, but he knew first-hand just how powerful the devil can be at getting us to believe lies about ourselves and about God's love for us. In an ancient letter, he wrote to a bunch of Christians in Ephesus, giving them some really practical advice: get dressed in God's armour. When we belong to God we have to get ready for the battles that will come our way. Paul is really clear that we are not to fight people, but to fight against the injustice, sin and darkness we see around us – all evidence that the devil is alive and active. Read part of his letter below on your own or with friends, and ask God to get you dressed up in his armour that will enable you to stay strong and courageous in your heart and mind.

God is strong, and he wants you strong. So take everything the Master has set out for you, well-made weapons of the best materials. And put them to use so you will be able to stand up to everything the Devil throws your way. This is no afternoon athletic contest that we'll walk away from and forget about in a couple of hours. This is for keeps, a life-or-death fight to the finish against the Devil and all his angels.

Be prepared. You're up against far more than you can handle on your own. Take all the help you can get, every weapon God has issued, so that when it's all over but the shouting you'll still be on your feet. Truth, righteousness, peace, faith, and salvation are more than words. Learn how to apply them. You'll need them throughout your life. God's Word is an indispensable weapon. In the same way, prayer is essential in this ongoing warfare. Pray hard and long. Pray for your brothers and sisters. Keep your eyes open. Keep each other's spirits up so that no one falls behind or drops out.

(Ephesians 6:10–18, *The Message*)

*I have always wrestled with what
it means to follow Jesus. Growing up,
religious jargon often confused, bored or
condemned me and I failed to see how 'living
for Jesus' could ever be a good option. Now I
know that my invitation is not to live a life of
restriction and dryness, but to lead one of hope,
liberation and socks-and-sandal-free adventure
with the fiercest man that ever walked the planet!*
Andrea Boden (Romance Academy)

*I became a Christian because I was blown away by the overwhelming
love God poured out for me, despite all that I'd done wrong. The
invititation of adventure to discover more and more of that truth
was one I could never deny or turn down.*
Dave Thomas (The Red Box)

Jesus, overhearing, shot back, 'Who needs a doctor: the healthy or
the sick? Go figure out what this Scripture means: "I'm after mercy,
not religion." I'm here to invite outsiders, not coddle insiders.'
(Matthew 9:12–13, *The Message*)

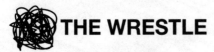 THE WRESTLE

You have now reached the middle of this book!

And, as with all mid-point moments, you have the choice of whether or not to keep going.

You might have grown up knowing Jesus all your life. Or you might be reading this book because you have recently decided you want to follow this guy Jesus.

But no matter how long you have known him, Jesus daily invites you to follow him – to see what he is up to and get involved!

My mum and dad told me every day that God loved me, but I didn't really get how good that was until I was about eighteen. I spent a lot of my teenage years trying to impress God and people by being Little Miss Perfect (while sneakily doing a lot of stuff I knew 'good little Christians' didn't do!). But all that changed when I was working in a really poor country, miles from home. That's when the truth of the cross really hit me: not only did God love and want to forgive and change me regardless of my good, bad and ugly stuff, but he was inviting me to be part of changing the lives of the people around me. Ten years on and I am still saying 'yes' to Jesus – and it's the biggest and best adventure I could ever have!

Beth Tash (Youthworker in Leeds)

Just before you get stuck into this chapter, think about why you said 'yes' to following Jesus. You could even write it down. Then read the chapter and let God speak to you about the kind of relationship he is inviting you to say 'yes' to.

I chose to say 'yes' to Jesus because . . .

_____

_____

_____

_____

The invitation's for you

Invitations.

You get them all the time.

Parties, weddings, picnics, detentions . . . ?!

Imagine you are in a science lesson and your attempts to teleport the school guinea pig into the English department go horribly wrong. Chaos ensues. Eventually you manage to put the fire out, but the lab technician still frogmarches you to the head teacher's office. You try to explain that you hadn't meant to kill the guinea pig but you still get into trouble, and as punishment you are 'invited' to take three days off school. Sounds great until you realize this is not a holiday but an exclusion, and the invitation is not one that you can refuse!

What kind of an invitation is that? It's a thinly disguised command that you have no choice but to obey.

An invitation is genuine only if the person making it allows the person on the receiving end to say no. True invitations have no strings attached.

Whether you have grown up in a Christian family or not, Jesus is inviting you to follow him – and his invitation is genuine. Even though he paid the greatest price in living and dying for you to make it possible for you to say 'yes' to him, he doesn't force or pressure you into anything. You can say 'no'.

And that's the risk he is prepared to take.

Jesus offers his invitation to you to know life in the way it is meant to be known. He invites you to get involved in his life, his dreams, his vision for this world. It is the most exciting invitation you will ever be presented with.

The wrong invitation

Have you ever been asked to go to the cinema with someone you really fancy? You get all excited about being on your own with them and in your daydreams you picture yourselves getting on really well, getting married, getting a dog!

You arrive at the cinema in your finest and smelling amazing, only to discover that the invitation you thought was just for you was in fact for everyone in the youth group. You read the invitation as meaning one thing when it meant something totally different – the person was just doing their job as the peer leader for the church youth group! OK, so apart from a bit of sobbing in the loos there is no harm done. But imagine if no one else from the youth group had been able to make it that night and you continued believing something about this relationship that just wasn't true.

Relationships that start on the wrong foot often end badly because they don't live up to our expectations. You may have thought that the person inviting you to the cinema was secretly declaring their undying love for you. The reality was totally different!

When you chose to follow Jesus, what invitation did you accept from him? Did you know what kind of a relationship he was inviting you into? It is true that Jesus is inviting you to live with him for eternity in the new heaven and new earth, but he has a whole load more stuff planned for your life right now. Does what *you* want for life match up with what God wants for your life? And if there is a choice between the two (your way or God's way), which will win out?

Refocus

If you were to ask anyone on the street what they think of when they hear the word 'God', they might say things like 'man with a beard', 'old guy who is a bit like Father Christmas', or even 'a good force in the universe'. If this is what they think God is like it's no wonder they don't see much point in getting to know him. But what about those of us who are already choosing to follow Jesus? Do we ever get the image of God a bit wrong? And does it matter if we do?

Well, in short the answer is yes – it does matter. Because how we see God will directly affect how we see our relationship with him. If knowing

God is just about a ticket to heaven, then we have missed the fact that he wants to be with us here and now, shaping our lives and helping us become more like his Son Jesus.

Some of us might feel disappointed with God because we haven't fully understood what he has called us to. We might think that God doesn't live up to his side of the bargain and so we feel let down. But has God let us down, or do we need to go back and take a look at what we believe about our relationship with him and maybe change our perspective a bit?

Let's have a look at different ways we might have *misunderstood* our relationship with God.

The 'bestest-buddy' God

The Bible says that we can be friends with God, but this is different from seeing God as just someone we hang out with. He is more powerful than that. We sometimes make the mistake of thinking that, if Jesus is just our mate, he must respond to things just as we do and and that he isn't any more able to sort things out than we are. If you think that Jesus is just asking you to hang out with him, then you might feel a bit put out when Jesus challenges you and makes demands of you.

The 'CCTV' God

So many people worry that God is angry with them. They think that what they need to do is keep God happy and then he will either leave them alone or stop bad things happening to them. So when bad things do happen to them or to people they love, they see it as a test or even a punishment from

God. The Bible tells us so clearly that God isn't waiting to capture us on camera doing something wrong. He is so generous and loving that he longs for us to respond to him out of love rather than fear. When we repent of the things we do that hurt God, others and ourselves, the Bible tells us that God puts it right out of his consciousness: 'He has removed our sins as far from us as the east is from the west' (Psalm 103:12, NLT).

The 'genie' God

The Bible tells us that God is OMNISCIENT (he knows everything) and OMNIPRESENT (he is everywhere all the time).

> I lift up my eyes to the mountains –
>   where does my help come from?
> My help comes from the LORD,
>   the Maker of heaven and earth.
> He will not let your foot slip –
>   he who watches over you will not slumber.
>
>   (Psalm 121:1–3)

Because this is such a mind-blowing concept, we can sometimes fall into the trap of believing that God only 'turns up' when we ask him to, as if he isn't already here. We've often heard young people at worship events exclaim, 'I'm just not feeling it tonight. What's wrong?' It's great to ask Jesus to come by his Holy Spirit to do things in our lives, but we mustn't treat God like a genie: 'We've rubbed the lamp and sung the worship songs, so why hasn't he shown up?' The opposite is true – God is *always with us*. The more we talk to God and spend time with him, the more we are able to recognize his presence with us wherever we are.

If you aren't aware of God's presence, it isn't because you need to do the stuff that magically makes him turn up to do the big and crazy things – it's because you aren't recognizing that he is already with you and wants to work in you all the time. All of us have to learn that God is as willing to speak to us on the bus and when we're on our own as he is in church services. He can speak to us through a Bible passage or through an encouragement from a friend.

The 'pushover-parent' God

Some parents think that they are loving their children when they give them everything they want. But it doesn't take a genius to realize that this can very quickly become disastrous because children don't always want what is good for them. Pushover parents find it hard to say 'no' and their kids find it hard to be told 'no' – even if it is for a very good and loving reason. Sometimes we can act like spoilt kids with God and get really upset or even disillusioned if God doesn't fulfil all our wishes in the way we want. This turns our relationship with God into a bit of a bargain: if I do this for you (read the Bible, go to church, not go out with a non-Christian), then you will do that for me (get me a part-time job, turn me into a worship leader, give me a great boy/girlfriend).

Reality check

Does any of this ring a bell with you?

Can you see how limiting all of these ideas about God are and how shallow a relationship we will have with him as a result, if we believe these things to be true? Misunderstanding who God is, and what he offers us, means that we misunderstand what our life with him will be like.

Time for the great news and the big picture, because Jesus invites us into the most dynamic, unpredictable, challenging and inspiring relationship you will ever know. It will turn your world upside down and equip you to join him in turning this world upside down. If that's not what you want for your life, then you might need to think again!

So how does the Bible describe what our relationship with God, Father, Son and Holy Spirit, is really like? God's Word gives us many pictures but we have chosen just four.

Master and servant

The Bible speaks loads about choosing the right master (boss) in life – and it's not just talking about your part-time job at Tesco. Our master tends to be the person, idea, religion or philosophy that we allow to influence us the most. It could be the money-master ('all that matters is that I get rich') or the popularity-master ('I need to be adored to know who I am') or even the religion-master ('I want to make it big in the Christian world'). But none of these masters has any idea how to give you the one thing you were made to have in abundance: freedom of life. If you think that you can get away with living a life without a master of any kind, the Bible says you need to think again:

> 'No-one can serve two masters. Either you will hate the one and love the other, or you will be devoted to the one and despise the other. You cannot serve both God and Money.'
>
> (Matthew 6:24)

Allowing God to be master of your life is the only choice that brings freedom and joy. He is such a great master that people throughout history face persecution and death rather than deny that they belong to him.

Allowing Jesus to be your master will change you because there will be demands made of you, the main one being that you choose to love God and his world with every ounce of who you are and what you have.

So Jesus invites you to give your own answer to the question, 'Who do you say that I am?'

> Simon Peter answered, 'You are the Messiah, the Son of the living God.'
>
> (Matthew 16:16)

Calling Jesus Lord and Master led Mother Theresa to give up everything and move to live with the poorest people. It's meant business people we know allowing God to influence *big* decisions in their companies, such as whether to open up their shops on Sundays.

What will it mean for you?

Teacher and student

A pastor once said that the church has got into the habit of 'warehousing people for heaven'. This means that we make people think that once they have become a Christian they can just sit back and wait to die! Nothing could be further from the truth. When Jesus invited the very first disciples to follow him, they didn't just sit around having a nice chat for a few years. They got on with the work of making other disciples. Jesus is a teacher who trains on the job! He got them healing people, casting out demons and even raising the dead – all without Bible college certificates and degrees!

> After this the Lord appointed seventy-two others and sent them two by two ahead of him to every town and place where he was about to go. He told them, 'The harvest is plentiful, but the workers are few. Ask the Lord of the harvest, therefore, to send out workers into his harvest field. Go! I am sending you out like lambs among wolves.'
>
> (Luke 10:1–3)

When you say 'yes' to Jesus the training and adventure begin immediately, and it's the *best* training on offer in our universe – or any other universe!

Lover and beloved

Jesus uses lots of different pictures to explain who he is and what he is about. One really powerful image is that of a bridegroom waiting for his bride. Next time you go to a wedding, watch the bridegroom's face as his bride walks up the aisle to him. Grown men have been known to cry when they see just how beautiful the love of their life looks as she walks towards him – it's an amazing moment and this is how God feels about us. He calls the church (everyone who follows him) his bride and he thinks we are so beautiful. In the last book of the Bible (Revelation) we sense Jesus' excitement at being able to bring us all home to be with him for ever, as his precious bride. The writer, John, encourages us to get prepared for Jesus and to welcome him as our bridegroom:

> The Spirit and the bride say, 'Come!' And let those who hear say, 'Come!' Let those who are thirsty come; and let all who wish take the free gift of the water of life.
>
> (Revelation 22:17)

Do you realize that God's first thought about you is love? He isn't exasperated, fed up, disappointed, angry – he loves you.

And his love is the most passionate force you will ever know.

Father and child

God is not a pushover parent, but the Bible does teach that he is a parent to us. He is referred to as 'our Father' and he also describes himself as a mother nurturing her children.

> Yet you, LORD, are our Father.
>   We are the clay, you are the potter;
> we are all the work of your hand.
>
> (Isaiah 64:8)

> 'How often I have longed to gather your children together, as a hen gathers her chicks under her wings, and you were not willing.'
>
> (Luke 13:34)

God our Father knows what is best for us and what will harm us. Because he made us he knows our limitations, so he gives us boundaries in our lives to keep us safe and also to enable us to reach our potential. If you have ever had to look after a younger sibling or cousin, you will know all about this. The child might not want to hold your hand when crossing the busy main road, but no matter how much he or she squirms, you know you need to hold on tightly.

There are times in all of our lives when we think we know what is best for us better than God does, and we might feel frustrated (like the little kid) that we can't do things our way. But the fact is that because God doesn't control us we are always able to do things our way. The problem comes if we make our own mistakes and then blame God for not looking out for us. God longs to be your loving Father. He is so eager to mother you and see you reach your potential. He also knows how hard you may have had it with your own parents – so like the best parent ever he will love you consistently and unconditionally.

Are you able to begin to trust that God always has your best interests at heart, even if it means you don't always get the answers you want?

Standing on the shoulders of giants

So it matters that you know what kind of relationship Jesus is inviting you into when he says, 'Follow me.'

The Christian family is the largest one in the whole world, and it is growing all the time! Throughout history, men, women, boys, girls, teenagers and OAPs have accepted the invitation to give their lives to Jesus. They have faced the same joys and doubts as you. Many have lost their lives for saying that they belong to Jesus – and in parts of the world today this is still happening. When you responded to Jesus and took your first faltering steps to follow him, you joined the greatest, most powerful army of light and love in the whole world. You stand on the shoulders of giants in the faith who have gone before you. And the way you live out your faith today will become stories to inspire the next generation to say 'yes' to following Jesus.

Read this report from a guy hundreds of years ago who wasn't a Christian, but was so impressed by how followers of Jesus lived their lives.

> Christians love everyone, and are persecuted by all. They are unknown and condemned; they are put to death, and restored to life. They are poor, yet make many rich; they are in lack of all things, and yet abound in all; they are dishonoured, and yet in their very dishonour are glorified. They are spoken evil of, and yet are justified; they are reviled, and bless; they are insulted, and repay the insult with honour; they do good, yet are punished as evil-doers. When punished, they rejoice as if quickened into life.
>
> (Letter to Diognetus, AD 80–200)[1]

What will the story of your life tell future generations about our Saviour?

This is my story

I _____ accept your invitation to follow in your footsteps.

In accepting your invitation, I choose to say 'YES LORD!'
'YES' to obeying you, 'YES' to following you, 'YES' to serving you.

Thank you for giving up your life on the cross for me,
for forgiving me and for filling me with your Holy Spirit.

This is my turning point and this will be my story.

From now on my life is no longer my own; I belong to you.
My future is no longer my own; I am running after your hopes and
dreams for me.

Help me to be obedient to the greatest law: to love you
with all my heart, soul and strength.
Help me to follow where you lead me: to serve my family,
my friends, my schools, my places of work, my community, your world.
Help me to copy your example in loving the broken-hearted,
befriending the excluded and speaking out for the voiceless.

I believe that I am involved in the greatest adventure this
world will ever know.
Give me a bigger heart so that I can commit to the big things
you ask of me,
and the strength to be faithful in the small things
you ask of me every day.

Master Jesus, I thank you for the privilege it is to be invited to follow you.
And I declare that I live to serve at the pleasure of the King of kings!

*I've decided to follow Jesus
many times in my life – as a child,
as a teenager who felt guilty for not
being good enough, as an adult who
struggles with challenging questions. I feel
like it's a decision I keep needing to make.
But the invitation from Jesus that I'm responding
to is the invitation to live life to the full, to see God's
redemption come to every part of this world that is
spoilt and broken, to work for hope and change.*
Jenny Baker (Sophia Network)

> Are you tired? Worn out? Burned out on religion? Come to me. Get away with me and you'll recover your life. I'll show you how to take a real rest. Walk with me and work with me – watch how I do it. Learn the unforced rhythms of grace. I won't lay anything heavy or ill-fitting on you. Keep company with me and you'll learn to live freely and lightly.
>
> (Matthew 11:28–30, *The Message*)

No easy answers

When I (Rachel) was younger I really wanted to be a genius dancer. Then one day, hey presto, a fairy appeared in the kitchen and gave me my wish in an instant. Ever since that day, I have been spending all my time dancing like, well, a genius dancer.

Do you believe me?

What about this one?

When I (Jason) was younger I was a bit of a school 'nobody' but I had set my sights on the fittest girl at school. One day she came up to me and asked me out, no strings attached. Then we lived happily ever after.

OK, so if this was the premise of a film you'd be either throwing up in your popcorn or demanding your money back.

Why? Because we know in reality that life isn't as smooth (or boring) as that! Life is more like a journey, with twists and roundabouts, lay-bys and diversions. Shakespeare got it right when he said, 'The course of true love never did run smooth.'[1] Love and life are both very unpredictable – which is probably what makes living and loving so exciting!

Our Christian life is no different. When we say 'yes' to Jesus, we aren't suddenly and magically whisked off to a land where nothing bad or difficult happens! Jesus tells his disciples this in no uncertain terms.

> I have told you these things, so that in me you may have peace. In this world you will have trouble. But take heart! I have overcome the world.
>
> (John 16:33)

It's a mind-blowing truth that you have been invited to be part of the biggest story on earth. It began when God said, 'Let there be light!' and will finish when . . . well, never. It's going to go on for ever!

It's God's story and, like most of the tales we adore, this story includes an apprentice eager to become a hero (you), and a master intent on training the apprentice to be better, stronger and cleverer (God).

And unlike the phoney illustrations above, this story obeys an age-old axiom (a wise truth) that can also be applied to real life: no one becomes a hero overnight.

Which is, fortunately enough, the title of the next section.

No one becomes a hero overnight

Everybody loves a good story.

Stories have the power to connect people, and occasionally they even tell us some pretty profound things about who we are and where we are going.

Think of three of the biggest, best-selling stories of all time: *Star Wars*, *Lord of the Rings* and *Harry Potter*. They all feature magical other worlds, but that's not the only thing they have in common.

The main heroes, Luke Skywalker, Frodo Baggins and Harry Potter are all quite similar. When we first meet them they're all orphans, living with an uncle.

They're all destined to be heroes, but they can't until two things happen:

1. They find their Obi Wan Kenobi/Gandalf/Dumbledore, a guide, someone wiser than they are, someone who's already been on the type of adventure they want to go on, who's faced life battles and has sometimes failed but more often than not has triumphed.
2. They go on a long journey (a character arc) that enables them to grow into all they can be.

God is your Gandalf

They all need a hero-maker, a father or mother figure who will act as companion, counsellor and, in reality, become their master.

This relationship is one of master and apprentice. An apprentice is someone who spends time with a normally older, wiser person whose skills they want to acquire. It doesn't matter whether it's a fantasy film, some martial arts epic, *X Factor* or a reality show on TV – the theme of apprenticeship is huge. Even over the past few years two films aimed at teenagers have been released with the word 'apprentice' in the title: *The Sorcerer's Apprentice* and *The Vampire's Apprentice*.

Realizing that this is how you should view Jesus –with you as the apprentice to Jesus as master – is where the adventure begins. God is your Gandalf and oh so much more than that. Not in a fantastical sense, but as part of the core story of your existence. People who have allowed God to be their master over a number of years can literally say, 'I don't know where I would be right now if it wasn't for God in my life.' This isn't some sentimental statement; it's a fact of life.

So if you're going to progress in life and especially in your faith, then you need to find someone or something that's going to take you to the next level.

We can make the mistake of thinking we don't need anyone: that we can teach ourselves all we need to know about life, the universe and everything. But would you let yourself be operated on by a self-taught surgeon who hadn't had any official medical training?

Training matters and if you want to be the best you need to be trained by the best!

Real heroes always travel

Doesn't matter what kind of hero you admire – a sporting giant, a military strategist, a scientific innovator, a faithful parent – none of those people took a pill marked 'instant hero'. They all went on a long journey to become someone that others admire.

You might be thinking, 'Wait a minute, what about *superheroes*? They become heroes overnight!' Well, we hope this is stating the obvious, but superheroes aren't real. Also most of them only get their *powers* overnight. Becoming a hero, someone who uses their X-ray vision/super strength/ power of flight responsibly, takes a lot longer.

The heroes in most stories have to undergo a journey of growth. It's what's called a 'character arc': a person starts out behaving one way at the beginning of the film but, often due to a journey of discovery, they end up behaving differently at the end. Like an arc on a graph, you can chart the things in the story that caused them to change.

So *Shrek* starts out as an ogre who just wants to live on his own, but due to his friendship with Donkey and falling in love with Fiona he ends up as a family guy who, although he wouldn't always admit it, loves having people around.

Often this will involve trials and an initiation. The hero-maker or master will train the hero or allow them deliberately to fall into danger in order to prepare them for greater danger down the road.

The Mr Miyagi school of discipling

One of the best master/apprentice films is *The Karate Kid* (we're talking the original here, not the Jackie Chan remake which should really have been called 'The Kung Fu Kid', but don't get us started). The film starts off with a mouthy kid called Daniel who moves to California with his mum. Unsurprisingly then he gets on the wrong side of the school bullies and, unluckily for him, they all know karate and are highly skilled in the art of making punchbags out of people.

After Daniel has been particularly cheeky at a school disco, the bullies chase him back to the apartment where he lives and start doing what bullies do best. The fun and games are interrupted by an elderly Japanese bloke who looks after the apartments. After Mr Miyagi gives the bullies a lesson in *true* karate, Daniel asks if he'll teach him karate.

Mr Miyagi eventually agrees. 'I promise teach karate,' says Mr Miyagi, 'you promise to obey, no questions asked.'

Daniel agrees, but no sooner has he done so than his master sets him a task. It's one of a series of tasks that have entered into movie legend – Daniel's job is to wash a load of cars but in a very specific way, 'wax on, wax off'. He has to wax on with a circular motion and wax off in the opposite direction.

Other tasks follow: painting the fence, sanding the decking and painting the house – all with a specific arm and hand motion.

The weeks go by and Daniel hasn't had *one* karate lesson. He's getting fed up. He thinks that Mr Miyagi's taking him for a ride and just getting him to do his odd jobs, so in a fit of anger he lets the wise one know his frustration.

That's when Mr Miyagi shows Daniel that all this time he *has* been learning karate; he has been making progress. He shows Daniel a few simple blocking moves, and when he's got the idea Mr Miyagi attacks him.

Daniel defends himself and knocks away every punch and kick Mr Miyagi throws at him – not a single one lands. All this time, by doing seemingly meaningless tasks, Daniel has been building up muscles and reflexes. His journey has brought him to a place of true strength.

Do you trust your master?

Daniel thought Mr Miyagi had got it wrong. He grew frustrated with his master because he couldn't see any real progress, so he questioned his motives and training techniques. Daniel's goal was to become a karate expert, but he thought that the path Mr Miyagi had put him on wouldn't take him there.

All Daniel had to do was to trust, obey and be faithful in the tasks Mr Miyagi had given him to do.

Many Christians make the mistake of thinking that, because Jesus gives us eternal life for free, it should be pretty effortless to follow him. Well, it's true that eternal life is free, but there is a cost to following Jesus. There's a cost for all sorts of reasons that we'll explore later, but in part the cost we have to pay comes in the form of obedience.

A master will always demand obedience. Why? Because a master knows exactly what obedience will produce in you. Mr Miyagi shows Daniel the results of obedience – the fruits if you like – and from then on Daniel is relatively happy to do what Mr Miyagi says.

If you haven't seen the results or 'fruits' of being obedient to Christ, chances are it's because you haven't worked hard at following him yet. The sign that you are following Jesus is that you are displaying more of the qualities of character that God is growing inside you. Only God can do this – but you need to put in the work of surrendering control to him.

> In your relationship with one another, have the same attitude of mind Christ Jesus had:
>
>> who, being in very nature God,
>> did not consider equality with God
>>> something to be used to his own advantage;

> rather, he made himself nothing
>   by taking the very nature of a servant,
>   being made in human likeness.
> And being found in appearance as a human being,
>   he humbled himself
>   by becoming obedient to death –
>   even death on a cross!
>
> (Philippians 2:5–8)

Our goal as Christians to become more and more like our Master Jesus means that we will be eager to display these qualities of humility and obedience in abundance. We basically say, 'Whatever our Master is, we want to be that too!' In accepting Jesus' invitation we are signing up to becoming his apprentice and following closely in his footsteps. We will always be working to become more like God, but we will never actually *be* God.

> Since, then, you have been raised with Christ, set your heart on things above, where Christ is seated at the right hand of God. Set your minds on things above, not on earthly things. For you died, and your life is now hidden with Christ in God.
>
> (Colossians 3:1–3)

It's a miracle to think that even as you learn to be more like Jesus, God through his Holy Spirit is working in you too. His commitment to seeing you grow in your understanding of his love is limitless.

 # THE WRESTLE

What are some of the 'fruits' that Jesus wants to grow in your life? Bit of a clue – they are probably areas that you struggle in! Take a look at the list below and ask God to reveal to you what he longs to grow in your life. Do you have the courage to say 'yes' to Jesus, your Master?

Humility
Gentleness
Patience
Faith
Courage
Hope
Obedience
Strength
Self-control
Peace
Faithfulness

Landmarks

Have you noticed how, when people give directions, they often point out landmarks? Places along the route that those who are lost can identify so that they *know* without doubt that they're going the right way.

'You need to go about a mile down here, then take the second exit at the roundabout; after that go on for another mile past a pub called The Green Man, then past a McDonald's and the road you're looking for is the next on the left.'

We've received directions like this when we've been heading somewhere. Often you wonder whether they're the right directions, and then you see the landmark, The Green Man or the McDonald's sign, and you know you're on the right path and so you *keep going*.

There are many landmarks on the journey to becoming more Christ-like. At the end of Galatians Paul gives a list of the fruits of the Spirit:

> The fruit of the Spirit is love, joy, peace, patience, kindness, goodness, faithfulness, gentleness and self-control.
>
> (Galatians 5:22)

In 1 Corinthians 13 Paul gives another list, but this time it's about what a loving life should look like:

> Love is patient, love is kind. It does not envy, it does not boast, it is not proud. It does not dishonour others, it is not self-seeking, it is not easily angered, it keeps no record of wrongs. Love does not delight in evil but rejoices with the truth. It always protects, always trusts, always hopes, always perseveres. Love never fails.
>
> (1 Corinthians 13:4–8)

If we're seeing these things in our life then they become landmarks telling us that we're on the right route. If not, we may need to check whether or not we're being obedient to Christ's directions. If we don't put Christ's teaching into action, if we don't forgive others, if we don't serve the poor and marginalized, if we don't love God above everything else, then we won't even get to those landmarks. We won't be encouraged that we're on the right track, and the chances are we'll turn back thinking that the directions were faulty, when, in all honesty, we never paid real attention to them in the first place.

We've been down this path. We've seen the landmarks and can tell you that a life lived following Jesus keeps on getting better and better. It's not without its difficulties but we do grow through them. No one becomes a hero overnight but it's all worthwhile in the end. Put your trust in Christ, be obedient to his teaching and what you'll become in the end is something so beautiful, so strong and wonderful that people will look to *you* to guide *them*. Along with Paul you'll be able to say, 'Follow my example as I follow the example of Christ' (1 Corinthians 11:1).

With the help of the Holy Spirit, you'll become a hero-maker.

Isn't that something worth paying any price for?

And now for the greatest thing of all.

Imagine that you commit to living this kind of life with all you have. You wake up every morning determined to express love and self-control; you go to bed every night asking God to help you to become more like his Son Jesus.

Even if you had this kind of total commitment, it would look like nothing compared to God's desire to transform you into being like Jesus through the power of his Spirit. That's why Jesus *sent* his Spirit. He is so focused on this and he has so much to give you, that he asks that you say 'yes' to him.

'Yes Lord, I am available to you!'

'Yes Lord, I surrender to you!'

'I can't do this on my own; I need you.'

And God replies:

'Great! Let's get started!'

> And I am sure that God, who began the good work within you, will continue his work until it is finally finished on that day when Christ Jesus comes back again.
>
> (Philippians 1:6 NLT)

> For it is God who works in you to will and to act in order to fulfil his good purpose.
>
> (Philippians 2:13)

 # THINK TANK

- Can you think of a time when persevering or completing a task has resulted in you becoming stronger or more skilled at something?
- What's the 'work' that Jesus wants us to do? Is it a tick list of praying, reading the Bible and turning up at church?
- How's your 'character arc' doing? Do you feel like you're growing in your understanding of God?
- Linked to the last question, have you noticed any landmarks? Are there areas of your Christian experience that you're growing in?

- If you could be apprenticed to anyone until you have all their skills, who would it be and why?
- We only want to be apprenticed to someone we actually want to be like. Was this the reason you started following Jesus?
- What do you see in Jesus that you like and want to be like?
- Which of his 'skills' do you want to pick up by spending time with him?
- What is it about Jesus' character that you want to copy?

You might have discovered that often you've felt most alive when you're worshipping God, when you're saying, 'God, you are so good; all I want is to do what you want.' Discipleship, following Jesus, is learning how to make that attitude real in every minute and every area of our life.

I grew up surrounded by the Christian world and all its supposed glamour. However, I only knew what it was to live fully for Jesus when my parents left me to serve him in the USA. Their obedience to his challenging call showed me what it was to love him unconditionally and led me eventually to surrender my life fully to Jesus on a park bench on my own the day after my eighteenth birthday.
Gavin Calver (Youth For Christ)

Then Jesus went to work on his disciples. 'Anyone who intends to come with me has to let me lead. You're not in the driver's seat; I am. Don't run from suffering; embrace it. Follow me and I'll show you how. Self-help is no help at all. Self-sacrifice is the way, my way, to finding yourself, your true self. What kind of deal is it to get everything you want but lose yourself? What could you ever trade your soul for?'

(Matthew 16:24–27, *The Message*)

The swap

There's an entire game show based on this next idea called *Deal or No Deal*, but we've been doing our own version of it as part of school assemblies for years (if only we'd copyrighted it!). For those of you who haven't seen Noel Edmonds in action, *Deal or No Deal* involves twenty-two contestants and twenty-two boxes. In each box is a promised sum of money which is only revealed when the box is open. It could hold 1p, it could hold the top prize of £250,000 or a series of values in between. The contestant brings their box to the front. They're not allowed to open it; instead they have to choose from the twenty-one remaining boxes. When those boxes are opened that prize is eliminated.

The contestant hopes that they will pick all the low-value boxes, the £5, £10, etc. until they're left with a high amount in their own box. From time to time a banker will 'ring' the contestant to make a deal based on the amounts that are no longer there. So if there's no chance that the player could win anything more than £20,000 as all the high-value boxes have gone, the banker makes an offer or 'deal' of, say, £8,000.

The contestants often refuse the deal, holding out for the box containing £20,000. They won't swap the box for the deal.

Our version is a little more budget than that!

We offer our contestant an envelope which they're not allowed to open, but we tell them that there's definitely something in it. Then we offer them a variety of sweets for them to swap with the envelope. First we offer a 2p chew; then when they say 'no' to the swap we offer a 10p chocolate bar, and so on. Finally we offer them around £2 worth of sweets for the envelope. Nine times out of ten they'll stick with the envelope, which in reality contains a bit of carrot peel.

It's very cruel but it makes a point – that some people live their *entire* lives like this. They're always holding out for a better deal, largely because they're unaware of the value of what they already have. Some people follow Christ like this. They hold on to Christ but, by the way they live and make decisions, you can see that they're holding out for something better. That could be *anything*: fame, riches, a boyfriend or girlfriend, a lover, drugs, the perfect career, a rock'n'roll lifestyle.

Right now you might be thinking, 'That's not me; there's no way I'd swap Christ for any of those things.' But whenever we choose the compromise over our faith, we're really saying that there's a better way to live than following Jesus.

Back to our budget version of *Deal or No Deal*.

The second time we play the swap game we do things differently. This time there's a £5 note in the envelope and, before we start the game, we whisper to the contestant, 'I promise there's a £5 note in here!'

So we go through the whole thing again, but this time when we end up offering the £2 worth of sweets they *definitely* don't swap. Why? Because they know the value of what they've got and it's clearly more.

Here's something you really need to hear: anyone who's unaware of the value of Christ will swap him for something that appears to be a better deal at the time. But there isn't one. Believe us, there just isn't a better deal.

I (Rachel) was asked to speak to over 500 teenage girls at a Christian conference, so I took a young woman called Vicki with me. Vicki had been a Christian for only a year, so I asked her to share her story about being found by Jesus. She was so nervous, but when she stood in front of the girls she looked at them and made this incredible statement:

> Some of you have grown up in Christian families and have gone to church from before you can remember – and you might be getting the feeling that you are missing out on real life. But I can tell you that I have been there and done that, and there is nothing better in this life than knowing Jesus. You can search all you want, but you will end up doing what I did last year – you will realize that knowing God is the best that life can offer.

It blew the girls away because Vicki had hit the nail on the head. So many of them felt that their Christian upbringing had prevented them from experiencing real life. They wouldn't have phrased it like that, but they had a feeling that they were living in the shadows. Hearing someone as honest as Vicki tell them that they had already tasted the real deal gave them a new confidence to go deeper in their relationship with Jesus. It doesn't mean that we should spend our lives in a Christian bubble or that we shouldn't have any doubts, but let's not fool ourselves that our friends who don't know Jesus are experiencing a deeper, more meaningful life than us.

Son of a Ford Mustang

There might be a whole host of reasons why people choose to walk away from Jesus, but in the end it all boils down to one thing: they don't know the value of what they've got in Christ.

It's a bit like two guys who buy vintage cars. The first is a car enthusiast: he's worked hard and saved to buy a vintage 1960's Ford Mustang – a rock'n'roll car if ever there was one. It's taken him ten years to put together enough money to buy it. But he hasn't just been working hard and saving, he's been building up his knowledge, buying maintenance books, searching online for tips, even working alongside a vintage car mechanic at weekends. Finally he buys the car and it's his pride and joy. He doesn't treat it like a museum piece; he drives it everywhere, top down, taking in the sun and the wind.

The second guy isn't a car enthusiast. He just wins the lottery and buys several new cars, one of which happens to be a vintage 1960's Ford Mustang. Which guy 'values' the car the most? They've both got the same vehicle, but who loves it more?

You could find out the going price for that car, and you could add £20,000 to that figure. You could go to both blokes and say, 'I'll buy the car from you.' Which of them would consider your offer? Which one would say, 'No way!'?

That's why some people walk away from Jesus: they really haven't even begun to value what they have in him.

We can get it into our heads that when Jesus was walking the earth anyone who heard him speak would have followed him for the rest of their life because they could see in an instant who he was. But that's not the case. In John's Gospel, after some particularly difficult teaching, a whole lot of people decide to stop following Jesus because they can tell it's going to be too hard. Watching them leave, Jesus turns to his twelve and asks them:

'You do not want to leave too, do you?'

Simon Peter answered him, 'Lord, to whom shall we go? You have the words of eternal life. We have come to believe and to know that you are the Holy One of God.'

(John 6:67–68)

Peter was beginning to realize who Jesus was. This revelation was a long process and his Christian life wasn't plain sailing – he denied knowing Jesus at his trial and managed to get into an argument with Paul over circumcision. But Peter's increasing awareness of Jesus as the Christ led him to be a key leader in the New Testament and resulted in him being martyred by the Roman army because he refused to deny the only man worth living and dying for.

This is why we need to realize that it is never our job to *make* people become Christians. Jesus wants people to weigh up the cost of following him. He gives them the freedom to accept or reject him. Although it must break his heart when people walk away, he allows it because his love is not manipulative or controlling.

Have you weighed up the cost of following Jesus?

Are you still waiting to suss out if Jesus is worth living and dying for?

There's a story about a Scotland Yard detective whose speciality was fraud. It was his job to spot fake money and he was unbelievably good at it. Someone asked him how he could tell the real thing from the copy. He didn't even need to think, but simply said, 'I spend so much time handling the real thing that I can easily spot the fake.'

So have you spent enough time handling the 'real thing'?

Have you really committed to Christ? Have you worked at your faith, or do you realize that you're a bit like the lottery winner with the vintage car – you've 'got' faith but you don't realize its value?

If that's the case then at some point you might find yourself swapping the real thing for the fake and not even realize that you've done it because you didn't know Christ's true worth.

Add it up

Jesus spoke about this a lot. He was like a guy in the market place, shouting out, 'Life and not just any life – *eternal* life come and get it. The best life available to humankind right here, right now.'

> The road to life is narrow – but Jesus didn't say it couldn't be found, did he?
>
> (Bri Draper, *Cherished* book launch, July 2009)

The thing is, Jesus never said that following him would be *cost*-free. This life is freely available to everyone but it's not free. There's always a price to pay. You pay the price when you respond to God's call on your life to live or work in certain places that don't always look great on your CV. You pay the price when you refuse to go along with fiddling the office accounts. You pay the price when you choose to save sex for someone you will be committed to for life through marriage. And the list goes on . . .

This is why Jesus talked about the cost *a lot*.

In the style of *Deal or No Deal*, here is the deal Jesus offers you:

Everything you are: every bit of hair, molecule of bone, all of your brain, every red blood cell. Every skill you have: your intelligence, your sense of fun and excitement, your passion, your loves, your likes, your dislikes.

And

Everything you own and will own: every piece of clothing, every gadget, every phone, every computer, every piece of music, every instrument, every house, car, dog and canary.

And

Everything you want to be: every ambition, every dream, every desire, every goal.

For

EVERYTHING GOD WANTS YOU TO BE!

That's the swap.

Deal or no deal?

It's not an easy choice, which is probably why we all struggle with it. But when Jesus says, 'in losing your life you will find it' (Matthew 10:39), he really means it.

Imagine you've got everything you are in a box in front of you: everything you are, everything you own, everything you want. Now imagine Jesus is Noel Edmonds. Hard to do, we know. But imagine he's looking at you and saying, 'I know you don't want to swap that box; I know that all those things mean so much to you, but as long as you hold on to it I can't give you the box I have for you.'

No one knows your worth more than God. God looks at your life and sees all the things that you think make life worthwhile – some of them good, some not so good, and some just plain damaging in the end.

But in comparison to what's on offer, the box you've got contains 1p. The box Jesus has for you contains the real thing, life to the full, life in abundance, a life lived in the heart of God that will carry on getting better and better, on and on into eternity. It's literally a price-less life!

So there is a cost, you have to give up the life you have now. When you think about it, it's not really a fair swap.

 **THE WRESTLE**

Here's something to do on your own to help get your head around the whole *Deal or No Deal* thing.

Get a box – could be a shoebox or any cardboard box. Write on it 'Deal: everything I am for everything God wants me to be.'

Then get a blank sheet of paper and draw three columns on it, with the headings 'everything I am', 'everything I own' and 'everything I want to be'.

Under the first heading write your skills, character, the things that make you *you*.

Under the second one list a selection of some of the things you own, including those items you prize the most.

Under the third one write down some of your dreams and ambitions.

Now look at the list you've come up with. You don't have to do this yet. Don't do it without thinking about it, but can you put the list in the box? Can you do it every day, every morning, every midday, every night? Can you say, 'Lord, your will be done on earth as it is in heaven'?

You might want to take this list and pray over it for a week or two. You might want to get some close friends and discuss the list:

- What do you find most difficult to give up?
- What stops you from putting it in the box?
- What makes you want to put it in the box, to make the deal?

Hidden treasure

Jesus tells a story of treasure hidden in a field (Matthew 13:44). A man stumbles across it and according to the law of the day he doesn't *have* to tell the current owner of the field that he's found it. The treasure is worth a huge amount and then some. So what does he do? In order to become the legal owner of the treasure the guy must buy the field. In Jesus' day land was worth a lot, as most people made their living from the land. So he has to sell everything he has and then he buys the field. When he owns the field, he owns the treasure in the field, and even though he sold everything to buy it, the treasure that he now owns means he's richer than ever.

That's a bit sneaky if you think about it. Shouldn't the guy have told the landowner he was sitting on a fortune?

Is Jesus saying that only a few people realize the true worth of following him? That it's like hidden treasure? A bit like the landmarks that show you're on the right path, it's only after doing the work of following Jesus that you begin to realize his true value, and, when you do, you make sure nothing stops you from following him. You devote your heart, time and energy to knowing him.

The hard sell

Remember Peter and the disciples sticking with Jesus because he had the 'words of eternal life'? Well, a lot of people realized there was something different about Jesus, that he had something different to offer. Not surprising really: walking on water and raising the dead are a bit of a giveaway that you're pretty special.

But people loved the way Jesus taught with authority as well. He wasn't just your average preacher; people hung on his every word. No wonder so many people came up to Jesus to say, 'I'll follow you!' They saw in him a hero, a leader they wanted to follow and someone who could make a hero of them.

But, repeat after us, 'No one becomes a hero overnight.' Yes, Jesus was happy for people to follow him, but he also told them that they had to be completely committed to him: they had to make the Mr Miyagi vow – obedience to the master.

We read this in Luke's Gospel:

> Along the way someone said to Jesus, 'I'll go anywhere with you!'
> Jesus said, 'Foxes have dens, and birds have nests, but the Son of Man doesn't have a place to call his own.'
> Jesus told someone else to come with him. But the man said, 'Lord, let me wait until I bury my father.' Jesus answered, 'Let the dead take care of the dead, while you go and tell about God's kingdom.'
> Then someone said to Jesus, 'I want to go with you, Lord, but first let me go back and take care of things at home.'
> Jesus answered, 'Anyone who starts ploughing and keeps looking back isn't worth a thing to God's kingdom!'
>
> (Luke 9:57–62 CEV)

Jesus tells the people who want to follow him not to expect a comfortable life. It's not going to be five-star hotels and limousines. And Jesus says that even if you've got big priorities they all come second to following him. In Jesus' day the responsibility of burying your father was a hugely important thing, but Jesus says, 'Following me is your number-one mission and everything else can wait.' You may not have done much ploughing, but the job was to direct the cattle who are moving the plough in a straight line, so if you look back, things are going to turn out wonky! Following Jesus requires all our focus.

Say 'no' to microwaves!

So why doesn't Jesus make it easy? Why does he insist that we commit to following him? Wouldn't it be easier if, once we've said we want to follow him, he just snaps his fingers and we're transformed into 'great Christians' who automatically do everything he says, without fail? Why do we have to work at following him?

Remember the vintage car? We truly appreciate something only after we've paid a price for it. If you've ever had to save for something you'll know what we mean. That's a big lesson in life – it's one of the rules of God's universe and we need to pay attention to it. The harder we work for something, the more we appreciate it, the more we enjoy it, the more we value it.

And Jesus wants us to enjoy following him, but we should also *value* following him like we value *nothing* else.

We are supposed to be the happiest people on earth! People who tell you they love Jesus but walk around with faces like thunder are missing out on the joy and peace that loving Jesus brings.

You might think that being transformed into someone who lives and acts like Jesus should happen in an instant, but that's the microwave version of spiritual transformation, and the Bible says that's just not the way it happens. We can think to ourselves, 'One of these days, one of those trips down the front for prayer and God's going to go "Hey presto!" and every-thing's going to be just fine.'

But if God just zapped us and turned us into the type of person who does whatever he says, he:

a) wouldn't have needed to send Jesus;
b) would rob us of our free will.

For God, it's all about his relationship with you and your relationship with him. Where there's no free will there's no relationship. God would be turning us into robots. It's only when we say we want to learn, we want to make our life's goal doing his will, that he begins to change us bit by bit by his Spirit.

It's a daily commitment, a daily desire to keep on giving our lives over to Jesus so that God can reshape who we are. When the disciples asked Jesus to teach them how to pray, he gave them a prayer to be prayed every day. The focus of that prayer was to do God's will:

'Our Father in heaven,
hallowed be your name,
your kingdom come,
your will be done
    on earth as it is in heaven.'

(Matthew 6:9–10)

We're a bit like 'living' stones in the hands of a sculptor – a perfect artist. Saying that we want to do God's will is like handing the tools over to the sculptor, giving him permission to shape us as he wants. If we trust him he'll turn us into something beautiful. Whenever we resist God's will, it's as if we are holding on to the tools, or worse, we want to do the sculpting ourselves – disastrous! Without God at work in our lives our transformation grinds to a halt.

And much of the 'work' that God requires of us is to surrender – to give him the space in our lives so that he can really go to work on us! That's where our transformation begins.

Giving God space to work will be costly, until we learn to love it. There's a famous phrase that anyone who goes to a gym knows only too well: 'No pain, no gain'. Perhaps a better way of putting it is, 'No resistance, no growth'. When you exercise by lifting weights, the reason your muscles grow is because you're actually tearing them! The resistance you have to overcome in order to lift the weight rips the muscle slightly. It's when the body repairs the muscle by filling in the hole created by the tear that your muscle grows.

So when you struggle to do God's will, when you struggle to follow Jesus, imagine that you've just hit a point of resistance and that, in overcoming it with the aid of God's Spirit, you're actually growing, getting stronger. That's one of the reasons why there's a cost to following Christ: he wants you to be better, to be stronger.

One of the biggest points of resistance you'll face is in trying to 'escape' from the fake life that's on offer now, the thing that distracts you from living the real life Jesus wants you to lead.

 **THINK TANK**

- Have you ever found any 'treasure'? Could be something you really wanted at a car-boot sale, a fantastic shell on a beach, a five pound note on the street. How much did you value what you had found?
- Think of a time when you really valued something because you had worked hard for it. Could be a school project, could be something you've worked at with family and friends.
- Have you ever given something up and later realized it *was* really worth doing?
- Jesus doesn't just ask, but demands that, if we decide to follow him, we must make it the highest priority in our life. Is he asking too much of us?
- What does giving God space to work on us look like?

*When I was sixteen I looked
around at the alternatives to living
in a Christian way. All seemed to fall
short for different reasons. Ultimately I
knew I could deny the existence of God my
whole life, despite the evidence of things like
an amazing creation, but I would still have to
answer to him when I died. I decided to live a life
dedicated to Jesus.*
Andy Patrick (Walt Disney)

> But now that you've found you don't have to listen to sin tell you
> what to do, and have discovered the delight of listening to God
> telling you, what a surprise! A whole, healed, put-together life right
> now, with more and more of life on the way! Work hard for sin your
> whole life and your pension is death. But God's gift is real life, eternal
> life, delivered by Jesus, our Master.
>
> (Romans 6:22–23, *The Message*)

More than a feeling

Has anyone ever told you about their first kiss with someone they really
cared about? If it was one of your parents then you might have run off
pretty quickly (understandably!), but if you had hung around they might

have told you that their first kiss felt like fireworks were going off and in the distance they could hear an angel choir singing – or that it was wet and a complete let-down!

Either way, the truth is that life is full of amazing moments and the older we get the more we experience them. We savour those times and think about them for the rest of the night, the rest of the week, the rest of our lives!

But no matter how great they are, we can't live just for the experience. If we did we would be disappointed.

So if we're always expecting 'fireworks' in our walk with God we might be disappointed.

You might have been to a Christian festival where you were overwhelmed by how much God loves you. Each night the worship time was electric, and when you went forward for prayer God's Spirit began a powerful work in your life. You might have experienced amazing times in your youth or cell group. People around you got really into praying and reading the Bible and it felt amazing.

Then somehow things changed and the feelings left you. Church felt like hard work: you couldn't get into worshipping God and the people around you seemed to lack the passion they once had.

You are not alone.

As you follow Jesus there are going to be moments when you feel God's power directly at work in you, and God loves these intimate moments with you even more than you do! But there will also be moments and seasons when you don't feel that God is even listening to you, let alone working in your life. The challenge for you is what you are going to do in these times, because this is often when the true mettle of our faith in Jesus is tested.

When we first decide to be a disciple of Jesus it can feel like a powerful first-kiss moment, and it's easy to say, 'You're the one I'm going to sacrifice everything for, no matter what it is.' But come Monday morning and the challenge of living day to day for Jesus, we realize that our faith needs to grow up and grow deeper. Expecting our walk with Jesus always to feel like a Christian 'high' is dangerous because when the feeling is gone we might think that God is gone too, and that's just not true.

God promises that he will NEVER leave you.

> God has said,

> > 'Never will I leave you;
> > never will I forsake you.'

> (Hebrews 13:5)

> See that what you have heard from the beginning remains in you. If it does, you will also remain in the Son and in the Father. And this is what he promised us – eternal life.

> (1 John 2:24–25)

Throughout the Bible God has called people to follow him through thick and thin, whether they're feeling his presence or not, to be faithful no matter what happens. The Bible is full of stories of people who, in moments of feeling far from God, experience his presence in new and profound ways. Sometimes God allows us to reach the end of our current experience of him so that we can move into a deeper relationship with him.

Jesus made this his very first point in his Sermon on the Mount:

> You're blessed when you're at the end of your rope. With less of you there is more of God and his rule.
>
> (Matthew 5:3, *The Message*)

We can probably all think of friends or family who seemed to be so strong in their faith and so on fire for Jesus. We might even have looked up to them and wanted to be a Christian just like them. And then they reach the end of their rope and walk away from Jesus. Some might even get to the point where they dismiss their whole faith as easily as you'd dismiss an infatuation with someone:

'It was just a fad, just a phase. I was young and inexperienced; that person wasn't *really* what I was looking for.'

Jesus wasn't really what they *wanted*.

There are many reasons why people walk away from Jesus: persecution for their faith; lack of growth in their knowledge; they just can't be bothered; or relying on a feeling that doesn't last.

But there's another reason which comes from not recognizing the value of what you've got in God: simply wanting other things more than you want him.

Jesus says that a big reason why people walk away from him is because, like a weed choking a plant, people get choked by worry and the pleasures of this life and so wander away. What does he mean? How can pleasure, which is surely a good thing, stop us loving God?

Jesus told a parable about this. He knew that lots of people would joyfully commit to following him, but somewhere down the line the joy, the experience, the nice shiny feeling would rub off and they would have to get on with simply committing to believing that Jesus is Lord in spite of how they feel.

It's the Parable of the Sower. Here's the version from *The Message*:

> He went back to teaching by the sea. A crowd built up to such a great size that he had to get into an offshore boat, using the boat as a pulpit as the people pushed to the water's edge. He taught by using stories, many stories.
>
> 'Listen. What do you make of this? A farmer planted seed. As he scattered the seed, some of it fell on the road and birds ate it. Some fell in the gravel; it sprouted quickly but didn't put down roots, so when the sun came up it withered just as quickly. Some fell in the weeds; as it came up, it was strangled among the weeds and nothing came of it. Some fell on good earth and came up with a flourish, producing a harvest exceeding his wildest dreams.
>
> 'Are you listening to this? Really listening?'
>
> When they were off by themselves, those who were close to him, along with the Twelve, asked about the stories. He told them, 'You've been given insight into God's kingdom – you know how it works. But to those who can't see it yet, everything comes in stories,

creating readiness, nudging them toward receptive insight. These are people –

Whose eyes are open but don't see a thing,

Whose ears are open but don't understand a word,

Who avoid making an about-face and getting forgiven.'

He continued, 'Do you see how this story works? All my stories work this way.

'The farmer plants the Word. Some people are like the seed that falls on the hardened soil of the road. No sooner do they hear the Word than Satan snatches away what has been planted in them.

'And some are like the seed that lands in the gravel. When they first hear the Word, they respond with great enthusiasm. But there is such shallow soil of character that when the emotions wear off and some difficulty arrives, there is nothing to show for it.

'The seed cast in the weeds represents the ones who hear the kingdom news but are overwhelmed with worries about all the things they have to do and all the things they want to get. The stress strangles what they heard, and nothing comes of it.

'But the seed planted in the good earth represents those who hear the Word, embrace it, and produce a harvest beyond their wildest dreams.'

(Mark 4:1–20)

When Jesus talks about pleasure choking us, does he mean that we'll stop following him because, as we've explored before, we think there's more pleasure to be had from other things?

'All means to attract and distract'

The above quote is from an early 1990s' rap band called The Disposable Heroes of Hiphoprisy – brilliant name for a group and even better music. Like a lot of good rap from that era, the lyrics weren't about girls, guns and money, but about serious social issues. One of their most famous songs was, 'Television: the drug of the nation'.

What they meant by the slogan 'All means to attract and distract' was that politicians and big business often get away with being corrupt because people are too happy being entertained to notice. People don't really care what's happening to others as long as *they've* got their video game consoles to play, their soap operas to watch.

They were right. They're still right. Ask any social campaigner and they will tell you that what stops poverty and injustice being tackled is apathy: most people are too busy being entertained to bother about serious issues. More people vote on reality shows like *X Factor* than vote in a general election.

Think they're wrong? Remember the 10,000 hours? That it takes 10,000 hours of practice to become a genius at something? Lets face it, most of us are geniuses at watching television and playing video games because we've dedicated a huge chunk of our lives to those pursuits. We spend roughly a fifth of our waking lives watching TV – a fifth of our lives watching other people live life for us. We're watching people live the lives we wish we could lead and we get addicted to it.

We may say, 'Hey, we really care about others; we really care about the environment and the global poor and all those issues that matter.' But remember about behaviour being belief? That how we act, and how we spend our time or spend our money speaks far louder about where our priorities lie.

This might be a tough fact to swallow, but if we prioritize entertainment then it shows that we think there's a different path to life, and life to the full, from following Jesus. Entertainment isn't wrong, pleasure isn't bad – but when it becomes the one thing we pursue, it gets in the way of the life Jesus has for us.

Different priorities of any kind can push the Word of God out of your life, and won't just stop you being effective for God but will mean you never learn to *love* loving God. You'll never experience the sheer joy of living enjoyed by those who dedicate themselves to loving God with all their heart, soul and strength. That's what Jesus means by pleasure choking us – simply pursuing pleasure all the time stops us breathing in good 'air' – God's life.

It's not easy to keep focused on following God when life in the Western world in the twenty-first century has so much pleasure to offer. In fact we doubt if there's ever been a time in history when a better fake life has been available.

Even better than the real thing

Ever thought of yourself as royalty? Well you are! You are a king or a queen, a princess or a prince. You might be thinking, 'Well, the last time I walked down the street no one bowed or curtsied.' But believe us, compared to how the rest of the world live, you and I might as well be royalty.

Ever heard of relative deprivation? Relative deprivation kicks in when you buy a new mobile phone, a *great* new mobile phone, and you're busy thinking how wonderful it is, then someone at school walks in with an *even better* mobile phone. Chances are you're thinking, 'I wish that phone was mine.'

You were happy with your phone until you saw something better; then you became a little bit envious. Relative deprivation means that you don't feel deprived or robbed of something until you see what you could have had.

A lot of advertising works on this basis. Your phone, TV or game console might be only a year old, but advertising does its best to convince you that you really need the latest version of that gadget, and aren't you a bit out of fashion?

So when we say you're royalty, it's because the vast majority of the world's population look at your lifestyle and they feel deprived. You might not live in a palace but, compared with how most of the world lives, you might as well. You have easy access to food, warmth, shelter, water, sanitation, peace, education – things that are just a distant dream for most people as they fight for survival every day. But the difference is that so many of them *really* don't have enough.

It's not only in comparison to people around today. Compared to the vast majority of people in *history* you live like royalty. It was only just over a hundred years ago that for the large majority of young people in the UK education was only a distant dream. From as early as five years old they would have had to work for a living in coal mines, in cotton mills or on farms.

In the UK today we're so rich that we've got something called 'leisure time'. We can spend, on average, one day a week staring at the TV or playing video games. It's a modern phenomenon that has actually made us feel more bored as a country – a state that the poorest of the poor never really experience! This really matters because leisure is all about pleasure, and the Western world is getting better and better at entertaining people.

Think about this.

You probably know people who want a career in what?

The entertainment industry.

As rock band Nickelback and hip hop band Cypress Hill sang in two different songs with the same name, 'Rock Star', you want to be a rock star, a film star, a pro footballer or something in the media so you can get *close* to the famous few or even become one of the famous few. 'Get famous' or 'get rich' seem to be most people's plan for happiness. Travis McCoy puts it best in his song 'Billionaire' where he describes feeling totally desperate to see his name in shining lights.

Yep, the Disposable Heroes are right: 'All means to attract and distract'. We live in a society devoted to distraction and we're getting better and better at it. Video games have more interaction, 3D cinema increasingly makes us feel as though we are part of the action, and phones are already an entertainment centre in our pocket: films, TV, games – it's all there.

So it's no wonder there's such a huge industry devoted to entertainment. The job of advertising and TV is to keep pushing the dream that in order to be successful you need to be rich and famous. It's a vicious circle that's hard to escape from – but there is a way out.

It starts with admitting that Jesus got it right when he said that pleasure will stop you being effective for God. You're so busy living the fake life – watching others live their lives – that it robs you of any ambition to devote your life to loving God.

The famous journalist, Julie Birchall, once said, 'No one who wants to be a revolutionary becomes an entertainer.' Would Jesus say that no one who is serious about building the kingdom of God gets *hooked* on entertainment?

The great escape

This is where the cost kicks in for most of us. All that stuff that distracts – you know why it distracts? Because it's fun, really fun. But you also know that it doesn't really satisfy. Ever spent an entire weekend in front of the TV or playing a video game, only stopping for a few hours to eat and sleep?

It's OK as a one-off, but if it's a regular habit you get that gnawing feeling in your stomach that life is passing you by. And it is.

So it's serious fun, for a while. And why wouldn't it be? Pete Grieg, one of the founders of 24/7 Prayer, says it's not as if the devil's going to tempt you to do stuff you *don't* want to do. 'The devil's not going to tempt you to sneak into a zoo and stab an elephant or break into the house next door and steal all the spoons!'[1] That would be easy to resist – unless you hate elephants and love your neighbour's cutlery.

The devil's much more likely to say that it doesn't make a difference to your walk with God if you spend more time watching TV than you do praying and reading the Bible.

But of course it does. Remember those truths in the last chapter? No pain, no gain; no resistance, no growth. Picking up your Bible instead of the remote control or the gamepad is a 'point of resistance' that you need to work at in order to grow strong.

If you were hoping for an easy ride following Jesus then it's time to get real.

There's a teenage boy in our cell group who decided that he needed to give up Facebook for Lent in order to help him find time to read the Bible. What a challenge! He found it so hard and really struggled with feeling that he was missing out on everything in his friends' lives – but he kept at it because as a follower of Jesus he is committed to doing all it takes to grow and be more like his Saviour.

Again, we're not saying Facebook is bad; we *are* saying seek God first over all these things.

You need to grow strong in order to escape the pull of the fake, otherwise you're going to end up with a Christian life that's seriously compromised, following God's rules only when it's easy to do so.

The Matrix is a film about a computer-generated virtual reality that keeps humans happy while intelligent machines use them as batteries. The humans think they're in a real world, but in truth electronic signals are sending a fake story to their brains. There's a bit in the film where one character decides he'd prefer the fake life.

The hero, Neo, eventually wakes up in the real world, a world torn apart by warfare where humans are constantly fighting for survival. Cypher is one of those fighters, who, like Neo, awakes from the Matrix and decides he doesn't like the harsh reality of the real world, so he makes a deal with the machines to betray his own race. Why? Because he wants his fake life back.

Here's the truth. A life lived loving God with all your heart, all your soul and all your strength is the *only* real life. Every other version of life is a fake. As Christians we're a bit like the guys in *The Matrix*. We've woken up to the truth of life and the fact that we are in the middle of a battle. And while following Jesus fills our hearts with hope, there's also a cost. We have to decide whether to keep following him when it gets tough or to ask for our fake life back. For many of us the reality is that at times we will hop between the two.

Being fully obedient to Jesus, living the only real life, does demand a lot of us. Jesus never said that following him would be an easy ride. Following his teaching wholeheartedly will stretch you in all sorts of ways. But, as the Bible points out time and time again, being obedient to God's Word and his law brings about the best possible conditions for growth as a human being.

But there's another reason God desires our obedience: he has a mission for us to fulfil.

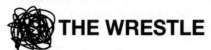 **THE WRESTLE**

RELATIVE DEPRIVATION: Take a moment to think about the things that you wish you had right now – even if you don't need them! Why not make a list? There's nothing wrong with these things, but we get it into our heads that we are entitled to have them because everyone around us has them too. As you write them down, allow Jesus to challenge your attitude to them.

_____

_____

_____

_____

ESCAPE THE FAKE: do you sometimes feel a bit like Cypher in _The Matrix_, hopping between a life fully surrendered to following Jesus and a life where you can't be bothered? Can you think of the last time you felt like this?

 **THINK TANK**

- Do you ever find yourself clinging on to the experience of a Christian event?
- How do you deal with the regular 'discipline' of following Jesus, even when it isn't glamorous?
- Not everyone responds well to the word 'obedience'. How do you feel about Jesus asking you to be obedient to him?
- What have been some of the 'fakes' in life that you have found yourself falling for? Could be an addiction to shopping, drugs, computer games, or a belief that you already know all you will ever know about God and you don't want to grow any more in your love for him.
- As a group what can you do to spur one another on to living your life for Jesus?

*I started truly 'following' Jesus
when I realized that the story of his
life, death and resurrection was such an
amazing work of art that no one could
possibly have made it up. That was the moment
I accepted his call to 'follow me' – and it blows my
mind to think I'm now invited, every day, to play my
very own part in that story! It's why I get up in the morning.*
Bri Draper (Echo Sounder)

> God can pour on the blessings in astonishing ways so that you're
> ready for anything and everything, more than just ready to do what
> needs to be done.
>
> (2 Corinthians 9:8, *The Message*)

Obedience is freedom

Ever seen one of those films where someone's caught up in a really
dangerous situation – could be trapped in a sinking cruise ship, on the run
from evil criminals or lost in the middle of a jungle. Then someone shows
up – the hero – and says, 'Hey, if you want to live, do exactly what I tell you.'

Imagine you are that character in danger. The clock is ticking, the water is
rising, the evil criminal has almost tracked you down. You are hesitant to

trust this stranger who looks like a cross between an army tank and a pin-up model, but you have a hunch that they're probably the only one who can get you out of this crisis. And your hunch is right – turns out they're a hotshot martial arts genius, an expert in surviving any terrain *and* they designed the cruise ship!

In fact, they're your only chance for survival. Obeying them will bring you freedom.

That's not a bad way to look at Jesus. He is your best chance for real freedom, so being obedient to him is not just a good choice, it's the *best* choice. Listen to the apostle Paul again:

> You know well enough from your own experience that there are some acts of so-called freedom that destroy freedom. Offer your-selves to sin, for instance, and it's your last free act. But offer yourselves to the ways of God and the freedom never quits. All your lives you've let sin tell you what to do. But thank God you've started listening to a new master, one whose commands set you free to live openly in his freedom!
>
> (Romans 6:15–18, *The Message*)

As we said right at the beginning, Jesus didn't only set us free *from* something (life without God now and in all eternity) but also *for* something (joining in his mission of making more disciples).

More on the mission later. But for now here's another way in which we can understand how obedience brings us freedom, and it's in the whole area of relationships.

We all love good relationships because we know that no one finds real freedom in life by always being alone. As the old preacher and poet John Donne said, 'No man is an island.' The reality is that we're never completely alone, and even people who like their own company rarely shut themselves off from others permanently.

But the thing about being in relationship, *any* relationship, is that you don't always get your own way. You don't get to do what you want all the time if you want to spend time with other people. If you always insist that it's 'my way or the highway – like it or lump it', people really won't want to spend time with you. If you want to have friendships and relationships, you can't be free to do what you want all the time. Surrendering to others is essential in relationships – and this is often the opposite of what we think freedom should be.

Everything in life is better when we experience it with others. Many people don't understand that and think they should be free to pursue their own desires at all costs. They often get what they want in the end – but with it also come loneliness and broken relationships. They find an element of freedom – but at what cost?

Only God gets to do what he wants, when he wants and, amazingly, what God wants to do the most is to invite others into a relationship with him. Jesus' life shows us this. With his freedom God chose to serve you and me, to look after us as a father cares for his children. Why? Because he loves us and he longs for us to love him freely in return.

Loving us is costly to God. It cost him the death of his Son and it causes him pain when we reject him.

Choosing to love is costly to us too.

Perhaps you know couples where one person puts in all the work and the other person just coasts, knowing they have a good thing going. They stay together because one of them is doing everything and the other person is too lazy to leave. They might think they are in a relationship, but it isn't going anywhere and it makes neither of them happy.

Sadly these situations are common. Most of these relationships or friendships will die out over time, because if one person is always giving and the other is always taking then love won't grow. There's a pop song by El Perro Del Mar that gets this right when it recognizes that you 'gotta give to get'. We can't just take and take, without giving back. In order for love to keep growing, we have to keep giving.

Jesus taught his disciples this really important lesson just before he went to the cross.

> 'As the Father has loved me, so have I loved you. Now remain in my love. If you keep my commands, you will remain in my love, just as I have kept my Father's commands and remain in his love. I have told you this so that my joy may be in you and that your joy may be complete. My command is this: Love each other as I have loved you. Greater love has no one than this: to lay down one's life for one's friends. You are my friends if you do what I command.'
>
> (John 15:9–14)

Jesus is saying that the best life possible comes from being completely obedient to God the Father. It's the most important thing he had to teach and pass on to his disciples. Why? Because the path of obedience leads straight to joy – 'that your *joy* might be complete'. Not so that God can enjoy ordering you about – what's in that for him? If he got pleasure simply from ordering people about, he'd use his angels as a worldwide police force and everyone would do what he said. No, Jesus wants us to be obedient so that we might truly honour God and in doing so have life and life to the full. If you really love life, if you really love *your* life, then start by serving Jesus wholeheartedly.

The door

The idea of being totally obedient to someone can seem restrictive, but try thinking of it as restricting in the same way as an entrance is. Imagine you come up against a wall so high and wide that the only way through it is to find a door. All your choices (flying over it, getting around it) are just not possible. The only way is through a door. But when you find one, you discover that on the other side is a world much larger, much more beautiful than the one you've left behind. How much would you care then about the fact that you couldn't pole vault your way in?

It's quite alien to our culture today that limiting your choices actually opens up life, but when you know Jesus you find that this is completely true! Choosing to follow Jesus and him alone leads to an appreciation of life that just keeps getting better, a freedom that nothing else in life can rival. When you fully experience the freedom that Jesus brings, you won't get hung up on the restrictions that obedience to Jesus demands. He has spelled it out for us: 'I am the way and the truth and the life. No-one comes to the Father except through me' (John 14:6). Jesus *is* the doorway to life.

Mission action plan

But there's another big reason why Jesus desires your obedience and it's all about the mission he has for you.

In *The Lion, the Witch and the Wardrobe* by C. S. Lewis, the evil white witch has been ruling the magical land of Narnia for a hundred years. She's cast a spell of permanent winter so it's always snowing, always icy. Sounds great if you like snow but she's also banned Christmas, the mean old hag. When the Pevensie children start to visit Narnia it signals that a change is coming: Aslan, a great and powerful lion is the true ruler of Narnia and it's rumoured that he's making a comeback.

What are the signs that Aslan is returning? The winter starts to retreat! The ice thaws, spring flowers start growing. Wherever Aslan walks, the world comes back to life.

This is exactly what happens when Jesus starts his mission. When Jesus comes to earth the Gospels make it clear that there's a darkness that covers the world: people who aren't living in the light of God are trapped in 'night' by their sin, which is rebellion against God's good rule. They are living lives that are in fact *anti-life*.

There are all sorts of hints at this in the Gospels. Matthew, John and Luke all point to the fact that the darkness, like the winter, retreats when Jesus shows up:

The people living in darkness have seen a great light.

(Matthew 4:16)

The light shines in the darkness, and the darkness has not over-come it.

(John 1:5)

And when Jesus is arrested he tells those who've taken him captive,

'This is your hour – when darkness reigns.'

(Luke 22:53)

Jesus knows he is about to die and he tells his disciples that his crucifixion is an act of 'darkness' – it's done out of ignorance and hatred, a lack of wisdom and understanding about how things really are in the universe. But God is about to make it known that he is in charge – Jesus will die but he will be raised again, signalling an eternal victory of his light over the darkness. It's not the devil's victory – it's God's!

In Jesus' ministry we see the darkness of sin on the retreat. He begins his mission by announcing that the kingdom of God is advancing:

'The time has come ... The kingdom of God is near. Repent and believe the good news!'

(Mark 1:15)

Aslan is here and winter is no more!

When Jesus set out, he wasn't on a cosy preaching tour; he was on a training and recruitment drive, recruiting for the army of light.

In John's Gospel Jesus says, 'I am the light of the world' (8:12), and in Matthew's Gospel he says to his disciples, 'You are the light of the world' (5:14). We are that army!

The only way we can escape the darkness is for Jesus to come and rescue us. The amazing thing is that Jesus then equips and trains us to follow his lead and work with his Spirit to pull people out of the darkness so they can live in his wonderful light.

We are in the business, to nick an idea from songwriter Bruce Cockburn, of 'kicking the darkness until it bleeds daylight'.[1]

What does that look like? In Jesus' time on earth it meant several things. At the beginning of his 'tour' of Israel, Jesus speaks to a crowd about the signs of his kingdom of light advancing:

'The Spirit of the Lord is on me,
    because he has anointed me
    to proclaim good news to the poor.
He has sent me to proclaim freedom for the prisoners
    and recovery of sight for the blind,
to set the oppressed free,
    to proclaim the year of the Lord's favour.'

(Luke 4:18–19)

We see Jesus on the move, gathering followers as he goes and causing the darkness to retreat. People are healed, the blind get their sight back and we see the servants of the dark, demons, fleeing when they hear Jesus' voice, just like cockroaches and rats running away when you switch on a light in a dingy basement.

The Bible has a word to describe what it will be like when people live in the light of Jesus' teaching. The word is *shalom*, which means peace, wholeness, nothing broken, everything hanging together. Jesus' mission is to bring this *shalom* to the entire world, when not just humans but every animal, every insect, every mountain, every tree, every star, every solar system will live in harmony with God and with one another.

We get a taste of this when we worship God and experience a peace and joy that nothing else can match. Jesus wants us to bring this peace into every situation. He wants us to experience *shalom* when-ever we feel like getting angry and lashing out. When people insult us or do wrong against us, he doesn't want us to plot revenge but to show his love.

And wherever we see brokenness in society, we are to repair it. We are to provide shelter for the homeless, restore dignity to the drug addict, and seek out the poor and needy and help them – the old people who need help with their shopping, the alcoholic everyone ignores, the immigrant no one befriends. We say 'no' to the darkness in Christ's name.

And it doesn't stop there.

God's mission is all about bringing 'spring' (his light and life) everywhere, so his mission for us is to bring release and freedom into every area of our lives, and through us into every area of society. That means if you are currently at school or college, ask yourself this question:

'What is God's mission for me today as I sit on the bus or in the classroom? Who is God asking me to bring release and freedom to today?'

If you start asking these questions every day it could mean that you will end up chatting with the one person at school whom everyone else avoids, or you might find yourself getting to know the dinner ladies and offering to pray for them. It could mean that you get a group of people together to serve your school in various ways, such as picking up litter once a week or hanging round the loos where you know younger kids get bullied. It will even challenge the kind of student you are. Imagine being the one person who is attentive in class. Being a follower of Jesus is not about sucking up to your teachers; it's about showing through your actions that everyone matters to God.

You see, being a Christian in school is not about just surviving, it's about thriving and doing all we can to make sure the people around us thrive too. As the guys from New Generation say, 'My school, my responsibility.'

So how do you take responsibility for changing the culture in your school or college? How do you and your Christian friends make your classroom a better place – not just for teenagers but for teachers too?

We heard a great story from New Generation Ministries about young people who wander into classrooms at break and ask, 'Who wants a free Bible?' So many people have asked for one that they regularly have to ask their church to supply more. Then there's the teenage boy who put a poster of himself on a school notice board which said, 'I'm a Christian, ask me why!' That week over 100 students asked him.

Every area of society needs the light of Christ.

So we don't get distracted, we don't ignore the cries of the world-wide poor. We study hard and study well so we can take key places in business, in the arts, in the world of politics or in social care. We use our creativity and practical abilities to offer fresh hope. We become compassionate friends and neighbours so that people feel loved, and some of us even train to be genius scientists and engineers so we can solve global problems that increase the divide between the haves and the have-nots.

> If one man or woman is willing to obey God, it can change the destiny of millions.[2]

 **THE WRESTLE**

> Jesus has a goal for your life; Jesus has a plan. He has a mission to fulfil and a role for you to play in it.

> Do you have a hunch of what your role might look like?

Many young Christians are so hungry to know God's plan for their life that they can become paralysed – fearful of doing the wrong thing. It's almost as if they are waiting for a direct angel visitation or words in the sky before they do anything! But you don't need to panic. God isn't playing hide and seek with you. If you are dedicated to finding out God's will for your life then you need to begin by recognizing that God's heart for his universe is written large on every page of the Bible. And his plan for you starts with you saying 'yes' to joining in his mission to put everything in this world back the way it was supposed to be: God in charge; God as ruler over everyone.

Now think about the different skills, abilities and passions that you have. Make a list below:

_____

_____

_____

_____

Why not find a friend or an older and wiser Christian to look over your list. It's a great idea to start praying about these things and surrendering them to Jesus. Allow him to show you how he wants to use your skills and passions to bring his hope and healing to others. Here is a list of great questions to help you think about your choices for your future. It is not a checklist, but a springboard to help you choose God's way for your life.

- Does this help me build relationships with people who need to know the love of God?
- How will this help me to grow in the skills, abilities and passions God has given me?
- Does this in any way go against what I know about God's mission?
- What do my family think about this?
- What do wise people in my youth group/church think about this?
- Does this go against anything the Bible teaches me?

Stormproof

Jesus wants to help you grow in maturity. He wants you to overcome obstacles and to wrestle with the truth. Why? Because he wants you to be stormproof, to be able to handle all the difficulties you'll face as his servant. Being stormproof doesn't mean that you will float above the world and not experience any troubles – quite the opposite. Following Jesus will open you up to a whole world of struggles – but with your feet firmly planted on the rock of Jesus, you will be like the house in Matthew's Gospel that is battered by storms, but stays standing, stormproof. You'll be like Daniel in *The Karate Kid* – able to defend yourself against whatever situation life throws your way.

Battle-ready

But God also wants you to be battle-ready. He has a mission for you to fulfil. God's kingdom is still advancing; his Holy Spirit leads the way but we still meet with resistance. We need to be skilled in the ways of love, compassion and justice in order to meet that resistance and break down its barriers.

We're a strange army. We don't physically fight, we don't use words of violence, we don't despise those who stand against us, we don't point out how wrong they are and how right we are. No, we want to recruit anyone who isn't for Jesus and we don't do this by criticizing or mocking them but by loving them. As the great preacher and church planter Peter said to the church in the first century AD:

> Through thick and thin, keep your hearts at attention, in adoration before Christ, your Master. Be ready to speak up and tell anyone who asks why you're living the way you are, and always with the utmost courtesy. Keep a clear conscience before God so that when people throw mud at you, none of it will stick. They'll end up realizing that they're the ones who need a bath.
>
> (1 Peter 3:15, *The Message*)

We must always treat those who don't know Jesus with the utmost love and compassion, because this is how God treated us when we weren't his followers. God could have said to us, 'As you've ignored me, so I'm going to ignore you.' In fact, he could still choose to wipe out the human race. Why would God take such a decision? Because if we carry on living without his rule then we will only continue to make this world a paradise for the few and a hell for the many. God cannot let that kind of injustice continue.

We may challenge God's right to rule, his right to make judgments, but look at the world we've created. Our societies are filled with people who are happy to forget the needs of others. We could make poverty history, as the slogan says, but we're not really prepared to pay the true price, which would mean a lesser standard of living for all those in the richest countries.

The human race hasn't done a very good job of deciding what's right and what's wrong. That's why we need to devote ourselves to following Jesus' teaching. We can trust in him and become part of his great mission to bring peace to every human heart, every family, every country.

What an amazing opportunity. God wholeheartedly desires our involvement in his mission. There truly is no greater adventure than obeying Jesus when he says, 'If you want to live, follow me.'

 THINK TANK

- Can you think of a film where the hero or heroine says, 'Do what I say if you want to live'?
- When is obedience freedom?
- Why is giving control of your life to Jesus not just a good option but the *best* option?
- What do you think it means to 'kick the darkness until it bleeds daylight'?
- What are some ways in which we can begin to 'kick the darkness' in:
    - Our streets?
    - Our schools?
    - Our world?

In losing yourself you will find yourself. In committing to loving God with everything you've got you will learn to love yourself. You will learn more about God's love for you, and that love will drive out fear and break down any hold that the darkness has on your life.

the REWARD

Give yourself fully to God.
He will use you to accomplish
great things on the condition that
you believe much more in his love than
in your own weakness.
Mother Theresa

> So we're not giving up. How could we! Even though on the outside
> it often looks like things are falling apart on us, on the inside, where
> God is making new life, not a day goes by without his unfolding
> grace. These hard times are small potatoes compared to the coming
> good times, the lavish celebration prepared for us. There's far more
> here than meets the eye. The things we see now are here today,
> gone tomorrow. But the things we can't see now will last forever.
>
> (2 Corinthians 4:16–18, *The Message*)

What's your reward?

I (Jason) remember one summer in the mid-1990s heading out with the
development and relief agency Tearfund to the Dominican Republic, a
country in the Caribbean that shares an island with Haiti. As you know
from the awful disaster in Haiti in early 2010, the area is constantly at
risk from devastating earthquakes. Our team's mission was to help build
a school that would be able to withstand hurricanes and earthquakes.

It required a lot of work, particularly as it was too expensive to hire big machinery like diggers and dumper trucks. We helped locals do a lot of the work by hand, creating foundations and pillars out of concrete reinforced with steel bars – all guided by a very wise, very funny (but very shouty) retired structural engineer from Texas.

One of our daily jobs was to empty rainwater from the holes we'd dug for foundations so that they'd be dry enough for us to pour in concrete. The problem was that, without fail, every afternoon there'd be a tropical storm that would refill all the holes we'd just cleared!

The work wasn't easy: the pump could get rid of the water quickly but it regularly broke down, so we had to form a human chain with buckets to clear the water out. Added to this was the fact that next to the site was an open sewer! Every time it rained, the sewer would overflow and spill water into the foundation holes. So we were draining sewage mixed with rainwater. Nice!

It was hard work but *good* work. Have you ever experienced that kind of work, either through volunteering or when you were part of a mission team? It's one of those jobs where you realize that the work itself *is* the reward.

Every day we played with the children of the neighbourhood for whom this school would make such a difference. Not only would it provide them with an education, but in times of extreme weather or earthquake it would provide much better protection than their existing homes. Knowing this was the goal of our labours meant that we didn't even think to complain about our workload: it was a real privilege working for those children and the town.

After a very busy four weeks we got a couple of days off. These were some of the best days of my life – we went white water rafting in the landscape where they filmed *Jurassic Park* and sunbathed on white sandy beaches. It was heaven. Building the school was rewarding work, but our strenuous efforts made our enjoyment of the couple of days off that much sweeter.

Working for Jesus *is the reward*

We live in a world that often sees work as a curse – something we've got to do to pay the bills or buy the things we like. But that's not how the Bible sees it. Being able to improve our world and one another's lives through the work we do is all part of God's plan for us. The Bible also tells us that, as God is Master of the universe, all the work we get involved in throughout our lives is done for him and to be a blessing to our community. He knows that working at something makes us appreciate life all the more. Seeing how little those children had and how much effort it took to build their school made me so much more thankful for everyday things we so often take for granted in the UK.

Have you ever been camping and ended up on the cooking team? You peel spuds for hours, wash up every pan and piece of cutlery going and eventually get to eat what you were so involved in making. And even though you are eating off a paper plate miles from home and it is raining, you have never tasted food so good! Somehow the hard work you put in to make dinner happen increases your own enjoyment. Strange but true.

So work is good, whether it is cleaning a shop floor or performing brain surgery. Work is a godly thing. This doesn't mean that all types of jobs or careers bring glory to God – that's something we need wisdom and common sense to work out. But the concept of work is a God design that we should honour, and work can be its own reward.

Jesus gives a strange picture of this in Matthew's Gospel. In one of those great invitation moments Jesus talks about what he's got to offer:

> 'Come to me, all you who are weary and burdened, and I will give you rest. Take my yoke upon you and learn from me, for I am gentle and humble in heart, and you will find rest for your souls. For my yoke is easy and my burden is light.'
>
> (Matthew 11:28)

Why is this strange? Because Jesus is saying that working for him brings rest. Surely work is the opposite of rest? The image is of being yoked to Jesus. A yoke was a cattle harness, something used to hold two oxen together so that they would walk in a straight line when ploughing a field. The farmer would walk behind guiding and directing the oxen and making sure they were ploughing effectively.

So why can work bring rest? How can it be its own reward?

Often how much you enjoy work – be it study, stacking shelves or ploughing a field – depends on several things: what's the reward, who you're doing it for, and what it's accomplishing.

What reward?

First up the reward.

In the book of Genesis Jacob (who becomes Israel) goes to work for his uncle (Genesis 29). He spots his gorgeous half-cousin Rachel and straight off says, 'I'd like to marry her.' In those days they didn't hang around when it came to saying who they'd like to marry, but they did have to pay a price – a dowry. A dowry is still required in some countries such as India today where the bride's parents have to give money to the groom's family. So Laban, Jacob's uncle, says to Jacob, 'That's fine – as long as you work for Rachel for seven years, *then* you can marry her.'

Harsh!

But Jacob didn't flinch; he just got on with it. The Bible says that even though he had to work all that time, seven years seemed like a day because his love for Rachel was so strong. Makes even Edward's dedication to Bella fade into insignificance, doesn't it!

I wonder if at any point during the seven years Jacob felt like giving up? I wonder if there were times when seven days felt like a year!

It's true for us too that, even though we know that 'good things come to those who wait', it is so tempting just to settle for nice things now. Remember the doughnut experiment? Young children being offered one doughnut now or five in twenty minutes' time? Most children in that experiment went for the one doughnut – happiness now. A significant number held out for the five though. Those kids who can grasp the idea that it is better to wait for a greater reward are more able to resist the instant nice nibble!

But what if you don't believe that there is a great reward in life other than what you can get for yourself now?

In the UK there are many people who work eighteen hours a day. They pretty much live in their offices and don't have a life outside work. Why? If it is just so that they can earn mega bucks to buy their mansions, second homes, cars, yachts, the works, then they are going to end up disappointed because it's all stuff they will need to leave behind when they die.

No matter how much you earn and own, you can't take it with you.

Jesus tells his disciples to work for a reward that will last for ever. It's a reward that we can experience now and in the future.

Jesus urges us, his disciples, to dedicate our hours to serving and seeking God's will because it will build up, like money in a high-interest savings account, to amazing *eternal* riches.

Our work (serving God with all our heart and lives) and our reward (serving God with all our heart and lives) are one and the same. The work *is* the reward – and it's the most valuable treasure this world will ever know.

This is part of our motivation to keep on doing God's will, because we *know* we're working for the fantastic reward of knowing God more and more as the days and years go by – and we *can* take it with us when we die. Recognizing the reward that awaits us can make our work seem light and easy. Rachel was Jacob's great reward, and all his years of hard work paled into insignificance every time he saw her.

A beautiful Christian man called Polycarp who was the Bishop of Smyrna in the 2nd century was arrested and in danger of being martyred (killed just for being a Christian). He had one chance of survival as those who arrested him told him, 'Turn your back on Jesus and we will spare your life.' The old bishop replied, 'Eighty and six years have I served my master, how can I turn my back on him now?'

For Polycarp, his love of serving Jesus was so powerful that even the prospect of dying couldn't put him off. He was burnt at the stake, but that didn't finish him off so they took him down and stabbed him to death. Eighty-six years of serving Jesus and, as Polycarp will tell you himself one day, every single second was worthwhile.

Which boss?

There's another reason why even the dullest work can seem wonderful – when you are working for someone you really like and respect. Think back to those children in the Dominican Republic. It was hard work and we Brits struggled to work in the heat of the Caribbean sun, but it was a pleasure working for the people of that town, because we knew that we were serving God.

The book of Genesis is clear that God created us to serve him and work with him in caring for the earth. In fact, God puts humankind in charge – what a privilege! Just like the angels, we were created to be servants of the Most High, an Old Testament name for God, and to be guardians over the earth and its creatures.

So the work is the reward when you are serving the right boss.

Have you ever had a job or been part of a team in school where you just didn't get on with the person in charge? It's really hard to enjoy your work when you don't respect the boss. So it's no surprise that people will take pay cuts and move towns or countries to work for inspiring and motivational leaders. It matters who the boss is.

Did you know that the team who serve POTUS (President Of The United States) don't get paid that much money? They may have been lawyers who were earning millions of dollars a year, but they are willing to take a massive pay cut to work at the White House – such is the honour of serving the President.

Your job in serving Jesus is much better than that. It is one of high privilege. Barak Obama's presidency will last eight years at most; Jesus' reign over the universe will last for eternity. When you wake up every day remember that you serve as part of a royal household, not just as a simple servant, but as a royal prince or princess. As the apostle Peter says in his letter:

> But you are a chosen people, a royal priesthood, a holy nation, God's special possession, that you may declare the praises of him who called you out of darkness into his wonderful light.
>
> (1 Peter 2:9)

In Jesus' and Peter's day the priesthood was charged with serving God in his temple. A lot of people today who study the Bible agree that the temple was really a remake of God's divine throne room in heaven. The temple even had a throne at the centre called the 'mercy seat' – it was a strong picture of how God's rule was at the heart of the Israelite nation. So the priests were a bit like the earthly version of the angels who serve God in his real throne room. Peter is saying that we now have that duty: we're all priests! We're all like 'special aides' to the president.

It's an amazing work we do and one that demands the respect it deserves. Imagine working for President Obama but not obeying him, not completing any of the tasks he gave you to do, taking 'sick' days all the time. You wouldn't have a job for long, but worse than that, you would have missed out on one of the most significant opportunities in your life.

We need to respect the job God has given us, but we should also take extreme joy in the privilege of serving the one and only master of the universe. There's a great phrase that the POTUS team use: 'I serve at the pleasure of the President.' Use this phrase first thing in the morning, *every* morning: 'Today I serve at the pleasure of Jesus Christ.'

What does this accomplish?

There's another reason why work is the reward: it's through what it accomplishes.

Everything we get involved with in life will have an impact on us. Either for good or bad. Practising a musical instrument, perfecting a dance move, training with a sports team at the weekend, smoking our way through our teenage years, all these things will accomplish *something* in us. Our experiences and the choices we make all have the power to transform us.

What things do you want to accomplish in your life?

Who and what are you choosing to be transformed by?

As we commit to working for God we're slowly being transformed to be more like Jesus (not the beard-and-sandals thing, but in character, heart and vision). This is another dimension to our motivation for keeping going in our faith. Being transformed by Jesus is the best accomplishment we could ever ask for. Not only does God by his Spirit transform us to be *stormproof* and *battle-ready*, but also to be *beautiful to the bone*.

What does this mean? It's probably true that most people are happy with beauty that is skin-deep. Even though we know in our heads that beauty is about more than how we look, who of us would turn down a chance to be a supermodel?! So why is this?

It's because people are instantly attracted to you if you look good, and you can make a pile of money out of it. But there are enough gorgeous people out there who are *abysmally* unhappy for us to realize that looks alone aren't enough. More importantly, God isn't impressed by people whose beauty is only skin-deep; he wants people to be beautiful through and through, *beautiful to the bone*.

One of the greatest prayers ever written is by the apostle Paul in his letter to the Ephesians, and it's a guide to gaining that kind of beauty:

> For this reason I kneel before the Father, from whom every family in heaven and on earth derives its name. I pray that out of his glorious riches he may strengthen you with power through his Spirit in your inner being, so that Christ may dwell in your hearts through faith. And I pray that you, being rooted and established in love, may have power, together with all the Lord's people, to grasp how wide and long and high and deep is the love of Christ, and to know this love that surpasses knowledge – that you may be filled to the measure of all the fulness of God.

> Now to him who is able to do immeasurably more than all we ask or imagine, according to his power that is at work within us, to him be glory in the church and in Christ Jesus throughout all generations, for ever and ever! Amen.
>
> (Ephesians 3:14–21)

Paul has a clearly plotted goal in life: to know more of Jesus at any cost. He's someone who's discovered all the 'landmarks' in the journey of following Jesus. He's grown in joy, peace, contentment, self-discipline, wisdom, and now he's intent on mapping out how other people can find their way on to this path as well.

Paul is really spiritually mature – how can we tell? *Because he loves loving God*. It's at the heart of all his letters: to *know* Christ and to *love* Christ provides all the reward he needs. But we know that this kind of love relationship doesn't grow overnight. That's why Paul is constantly praying for the churches he's helped to build up – that God's Spirit might lead them into a greater knowledge and love of Jesus.

It's a love so great that it can't be contained, and Paul wants us to understand just how big it is – 'how wide and long and high and deep is the love of Christ'! The love of Christ is so immense – like an entire country, an entire universe that you can spend an eternity journeying deeper into! By following in the footsteps of disciples like Paul, we can work at becoming beautiful to the bone.

A friend of ours once described what's going on in this passage as a little bit like seeing your life as a home that God moves into.

Some people might choose to move into a show house that is already fully equipped with furniture and funky decor. But most people move into an older house that might need some work to make it feel like theirs. To start with the house isn't ideal, but bit by bit, year by year, the family make the house *their* home, with the furniture they like, decorations they love. The longer they live in it the more they make it their own.

Being a Christian is about working with the Spirit to make changes to yourself so that Jesus feels more at home in your life. This is what Paul is getting at when he says:

> I pray that out of his glorious riches he may strengthen you with power through his Spirit in your inner being, so that Christ may dwell in your hearts through faith.
>
> (Ephesians 3:16–17)

When we become Christians Jesus doesn't snap his fingers and turn our lives into a sparkling new 'show house'! We are more like an old home that Jesus moves into, and his Holy Spirit is the best interior decorator in the business. Over time the 'home' is transformed as we invite God's Spirit to work in our life. As Paul says, God's desire is that all his fullness lives in you. That's a mind-blowing idea: God wants increasingly to fill you with his love, joy, peace, wisdom, power.

Amazing!

Some Christians never give God permission to do this transformational work. They don't trust that God will make changes that they'll not only like but *love!* They are fond of the old furniture and decorations just the way they are, or they are afraid of the mess that is created by home improvements. Effectively they're saying Jesus can do what he likes in the garage of their lives or in the porch, but the bulk of the house is off-limits.

We don't want that to be us, or you!

Becoming more Jesus-like takes work, but it's essential for us to be all that we can be as his disciples. It's exciting to allow God to make all the changes he sees fit in our lives – who knows where it might lead?

 **THE WRESTLE**

Think about what areas of your life are currently off-limits to God and the work of his Spirit. It might be school, studies, future plans, sexuality, friends, family, how you spend your leisure time.

God doesn't want to do a whirlwind decoration job on your house, but he does demand to be the guy in charge. He knows what changes need to take place and how to make those changes, and he'll do them bit by bit as you give every area of your life to him.

How would you now answer the three questions posed at the beginning of this chapter:

1. What's the reward you're looking for?
2. Who are you working for?
3. What is your work accomplishing?

Things will only get better

The most important choice you will ever make is to be a disciple of Jesus. It's the greatest challenge you will ever face.

But with the help of God's Spirit and a few sage warriors (wise Christian friends) you can RISE to it. You can fully trust that God will supply everything you need as you depend on him and seek to be obedient to him in every area of your life.

Christ's goal is to see you become *stormproof*, *battle-ready* and *beautiful to the bone*: that with every molecule and ounce of your one wild and precious life you will live to serve him. We hope this book has helped you begin to map how that can happen in your life.

As you follow Jesus, we pray that you will know more and more of the truth that King David discovered when he sang to God:

> You make known to me the path of life;
>> you will fill me with joy in your presence,
>> with eternal pleasures at your right hand.

(Psalm 16:11)

The path of life, that's what we're walking on when we follow Jesus. It's a path that's always rising, always heading up, often difficult to follow, but one that we are so eager to explore as Jesus helps us understand the true nature of the rewards that await us in this life and the next.

Life: the remix

The Bible speaks of a future life in heaven that's not about sitting around on clouds playing harps! The picture is of a new heaven and a new earth where we'll be working as one team: God the Father, God the Son, God the Holy Spirit, all the angels and all those humans who've followed Christ, taking care of our brand-new, remixed universe.

What will it be like?

Did you know that scientists keep on finding more and more planets in the universe – billions of them. What if, when God reworks everything, all the planets are habitable? What if God gives you an entire planet to be in charge of? You and a few hundred friends and a team of angels spend a thousand years making your planet look fantastic, redirecting rivers, building cities in the tops of trees, channelling the power of volcanoes! Then you get to travel around the rest of the universe seeing what other people have done with their planets.

OK, so there is no proof in the Bible for any of this! But just imagine what kind of possibilities an existence with God for all eternity will throw at us.

Yeehaaah!

One thing we can be totally sure of is that God's got a beautiful future planned for us. That's why Jesus went to the cross. He suffered because he knew what his task would accomplish for us:

> Jesus . . . who for the joy set before him endured the cross.
>
> (Hebrews 12:2)

For the joy of all creation (animals, people, angels) living together in perfect harmony for ever with God. No more tears, no more suffering, just the beautiful truth of us all setting sail together towards horizons of more love, more peace, more adventure.

What an amazing hope we have. In the light of this reward, in the light of what a pleasure and privilege it is to serve Jesus, we can say with Paul:

> Everything else is worthless when compared with the infinite value of knowing Christ my Lord.
>
> (Philippians 3:8, NLT)

It's not easy to follow Christ, but with the aid of God's Spirit you *can* RISE to the challenge. If you devote your heart to serving God there are no limits to what you can achieve in his name and for his glory. If you're looking for the next step then head to The Workout, but for now this is the prayer we'd love you to pray with us:

> Holy Father,
> Before you called us,
> before you made your love known to us,
> we had no idea what it meant to be truly alive.
>
> But through your Son Jesus we have begun to taste life and we
> want more.

We know that we can only make our way further into your love,
further into life in all its fullness,
by serving you wholeheartedly,
by holding nothing back,
by allowing your will to be done in every area of our lives.

But we know to make you first in our lives is a wrestle. It's a
struggle and we need your strength. Please send us your
Spirit, day by day, hour by hour, minute by minute to
guide us, to encourage us, to give us wisdom and strength.

Use us as you choose so that men, women and children all over
this world will come to love you and serve you as Lord.

Jesus we RISE to the challenge of following you.
We throw our hearts wide open to say that we trust you.
We surrender our hopes, dreams and ambitions to you
and we choose to embrace all you have for us.
We invite you to make us whole and to lead us deeper into the
greatest adventure the universe has ever known.
May we RISE to the challenge of being your followers,
And may our praise to you RISE up for ever.

AMEN

God is strong, and he wants
you strong. So take everything the
Master has set out for you, well-made
weapons of the best materials. And put
them to use so that you will be able to stand
against everything the Devil throws your way.
This is no afternoon athletic contest that we'll walk
away from and forget about in a couple of hours.
This is for keeps, a life-or-death fight to the finish
against the Devil and all his angels.
(Ephesians 6:10–12, The Message)

Stretch

If *RISE* has stretched your brain then great, but that wasn't our main goal. If *RISE* has challenged you to do things for God then wonderful, but that wasn't our chief goal either.

So what were we after?

Remember the greatest law in the universe: 'Love the Lord your God with all your heart, with all your soul and with all your strength.' That's our goal, because when we do this it leads us to an amazing place – spiritual maturity. We can associate maturity with being old and sensible, but the biblical picture is one of small tree versus big tree: the more we commit ourselves to following God, the bigger and stronger we become.

We've described being spiritually mature as being *stormproof*, *battle-ready* and *beautiful to the bone*, but we also think that the way you can really tell that you're growing in your faith is that you increasingly *love loving God*.

There are times when we're overwhelmed by our sense of love for God, but we're not just talking about an occasional experience: we're talking about a life where every waking moment is filled with a rich sense of love for God. The beauty of Jesus giving us his Spirit is that we don't have to wait until the new heaven and new earth for that kind of relationship – we can have it right here, right now.

But it's going to take a little 'wax on, wax off' action because it's a journey we need to travel and it's going to take work on our behalf. We can't be disciples without discipline. Which simply means that we need to dedicate ourselves to learning from the Master.

Be assured of this though, discipline always reaps results. Not only that, but discipline will *fuel* our desire for God.

So what kind of discipline? What kind of 'regular' work will start us on that path to love loving God?

First we'll give you some principles about growing in God and then you can choose your own 'wax on, wax off' activities – workouts that will help you focus and develop spiritual 'muscle'.

Growing in God

'Make space for space!' Remember the image of the sculptor? That you're like a bit of living rock that allows a brilliant artist to work on you? One of the most important things to recognize about giving time to God is that we're giving him space to work on us. Whether it's praying or reading the Bible, going for a walk with just us, God and the dog, we're saying that, bit by bit, we want God to shape and transform us. Remember, if we don't give God space to work we'll see little change in our lives.

Giving God space, whether we're on the train, on our lunch, or white water rafting, is about asking God to teach us – it's sitting at the feet of the Master.

'Don't try to be a hero overnight!' After being challenged about becoming more disciplined in the way we seek God, the temptation is to go for it all at once – get up at 5am every morning, read 400 chapters of the Bible every day, fast for three weeks in a row!

While it is really important to set a rhythm in the way we make space in our lives, don't start trying to learn on a full drum kit! Begin with a gentle beat at first: why not try 'bookending' your day with God? If you're not used to praying regularly day in day out, then start by giving God five minutes at the beginning of your day and five minutes at the end of your day.

If you were taking up weight lifting you'd be really put off if you tried to lift 100 kilogrammes straightaway! Start with small weights at first, then build your way up.

'Don't let distractions distract you' Chances are that when you give God space to work, your head will get filled with all sorts of other stuff – the sudden urge to clip your toenails or rearrange your sock drawer. Let's face it, our heads get filled with so many fantastic things every day that it's often hard to focus. Don't be put off if you get distracted, and remember that you're starting by *learning* how to focus on God. It can be helpful to start with a centring prayer or Bible meditation (see below).

'Learn the rules so you can break the rules' We might be tempted to think that seeking God doesn't have to be about a set time and place every day; we might think we want to seek God while hang-gliding or manicuring the cat. Of course you can seek God in many different ways and at all times, but building something regular into our days is the best way to start. Remember that being in relationship with God means choosing Christ as Lord, and that means surrendering our time so that we make seeking God a priority.

Then, when you begin to *love loving God* you'll become more and more aware of God's presence with you at all times. You'll realize that, whether you're completing homework, training for a triathlon or solving the world's water crisis, all of life is a partnership with God. God working with you, you working for God.

'Remember to wrestle' This isn't going to be easy but remember that the wrestle is worth it. Whenever you think, 'This is too difficult; I can't keep this up; I don't want to keep this up', then take a deep breath and ask God to help you wrestle. Remember, it's at the points of resistance that we grow.

Workouts

Here are some ideas for how you can begin to give God all of you, bit by bit.

1. Love God, love the Word

Has anyone ever given you a biography of a hero of yours? A sports star like Dame Kelly Holmes, a history changer like Martin Luther King or an actor like Will Smith? You probably couldn't put it down.

The Bible is clearly the story of God, the story of the greatest hero the universe has ever known. It's a big story and one that's not always easy to understand, but we need to if we're going to develop our love of Jesus.

There aren't any *easy* ways to read the Bible, but there are plenty of creative ways of connecting with it.

We suggest you start by getting to know one bit of it really well. Take the Gospel of Mark which has only sixteen chapters and read through it in one evening. Alternatively listen to it on audio. Learn to wrestle with it, write down any questions you have and then ask a parent or church leader to answer them. After all, Jesus did most of his teaching by responding to questions.

When you feel ready you can start a reading plan, working through the whole Bible in a year.

A really great idea is to download Scripture on to your phone so that you can read it wherever you are.

For more suggestions and other resources take a look at:

www.soulsurvivor.com/uk/soulfood/bible/index.html –
a daily Bible reading.

www.biblefresh.com/ –
plenty of up-to-date information and suggestions.

www.youversion.com/mobile –
download the Bible on to your mobile device.

www.zgraphicnovels.com/series/mangaBible.php –
the Bible as a series of Manga graphic novels.

2. Centring prayers and meditation

A great way to learn to focus on God and become more aware of his presence is through simple meditation and centring prayers. You can take just one word like 'Jesus' or a simple line from the Bible such as,

Acknowledge and take to heart this day that the Lord is God in heaven above and on the earth below.

(Deuteronomy 4:39)

Or

Be still, and know that I am God.

(Psalm 46:10)

Begin by asking God to make you more aware of his presence. Relax by putting on some chilled music or simply breathing deeply. You can then repeat the word or line, using it to worship God. Try finding your own rhythm, perhaps breathing in deeply and then speaking the word or line as you breathe out, either aloud or in your head. Make sure there's space between the times you read it out.

If you get distracted you can use a simple word or line to 'centre' yourself back on God. It's a really good practice to begin with. Remember that you're not waiting for God to show up in a burst of fireworks! You're simply learning to wait at the feet of the Master. It's part of how we learn obedience.

Alternatively, you can do *lectio divina* or 'divine reading' – a meditation based on small chunks of the Bible. Find out more about it here:

   www.biblesociety.org.uk/products/1265/49/lectio_divina_english_
   june_august_2010/

3. Groups are great

Why not get two friends to join with you in regular prayer or Bible study? That way you can help one another to focus. Or you could create an online group dedicated to a spiritual adventure. Our youth group recently decided to read through the Bible in a year and we created a Facebook group to encourage one another, make comments and ask questions.

4. Practise regular acts of kindness

Random acts of kindness are wonderful, but even better is dedicating yourself to helping someone out on a regular basis. Why not volunteer to DJ at a local hospital, play Scrabble down at an old people's home or shop for someone who has difficulty getting out of the house? Ask your church/youth leader for suggestions. There are a million ways you could think of to help people. What's really important is that you choose something and stick with it.

As well as physically helping people out, why not choose a campaign to get involved in? Again you'll learn so much if you stick with it rather than making it a one-off thing.

Here are some helpful websites. Why not find out about any campaigns your church, school or local charities are involved in?

http://youth.tearfund.org/

http://www.stopthetraffik.org/

http://www.soulsurvivor.com/uk/soulfood/news/index.html

5. Find your Gandalf

This is really important. You don't have to find someone with a beard down to their ankles and a pointy hat but, if that's what your church leader looks like, fair enough. Do find someone a little older and wiser who's prepared to meet up with you in a public place (coffee shops are great!) at least once a month, to spur you on in your journey of growth. They can encourage you to set targets, help you with those difficult Bible passages and they might even buy you a white chocolate and raspberry muffin from time to time. Ask your church or youth leader to suggest someone. If there's a few of you who would like a mentor, then your church could organize some training for adults in your congregation. If so you could suggest they get in touch with:

Jon Langford at www.stpaulssalisbury.org/

The Sophia Network provides great mentoring training (blog. sophianetwork.org.uk/mentoring.html), as do many of the organizing bodies for the main church denominations.

6. Love loving God and love loving your church

When it comes to loving God, family is really important. In order to grow in faith we need to love the family that Jesus has put us in – the family of God. In fact, in many ways being a Christian means treating this random bunch of people we meet with weekly as if they were *close* family.

Think about that. In families we pull together as a team so that no individual ends up doing all the work. It should be the same in church. In families we celebrate anniversaries and throw parties when brothers, sisters, mums and dads have achieved something fantastic. It should be the same in church. In families we should be quick to forgive because we have to live with the people who've offended us. It's the same in church. In families we learn together, work together, play together, eat together. It should be the same . . . well you know!

Being a committed member of the church is how we learn to serve Christ well. Let's not wait to be given a task or asked for help. Let's ask our youth and church leaders what we can do to help out. And let's not just look for the stuff we like to do, such as singing in the band. Let's ask if there's something practical we can do first, like showing up early to arrange the chairs or set up the PA system, or helping out at a meal for the elderly. Maybe you could even think about giving regularly to the work of the church.

Remember that God loves his church and so should we. There are few better 'workouts' for our faith than realizing we have a part to play in the family of faith, whatever age we are.

Keep handling the good stuff

These ideas are just for starters. Being a disciple of Jesus means that we're lifelong learners, focused on applying what God has to teach us in every area of life. However you decide to deepen your walk with God, we hope that you'll handle so much of the real life that God has on offer that you'll learn to spot the fake life a mile off.

Notes

two: the PLAN
1. From 'Nature Boy', written by Eden Ahbez and performed by Nat King Cole.

three: the MYSTERY
1. *The Collected Poems of Ted Hughes* (Faber and Faber Ltd, 2005). Used by permission.

five: the INVITATION
1. Taken from Alan Hirsch with Darryn Altclass, *The Forgotten Ways Handbook: A Practical Guide for Developing Missional Churches* (Brazos Press, 2009).

six: the JOURNEY
1. Lysander in *A Midsummer Night's Dream*, Act 1, Scene 1.

eight: the ESCAPE
1. Youthwork Conference, 2009.

nine: the MISSION
1. 'Lovers in a Dangerous Time' by Bruce Cockburn (1984).
2. D. C. Talks and the Voice of the Martyrs, *Jesus Freaks: Stories of Those Who Stood for Jesus, the Ultimate Jesus Freaks* (Albury, 1999).